FOREIGN INFLUENCES IN ELIZABETHAN PLAYS

FOREIGN INFLUENCES IN ELIZABETHAN PLAYS

BY

FELIX E. SCHELLING

PROFESSOR OF ENGLISH LITERATURE IN
THE UNIVERSITY OF PENNSYLVANIA

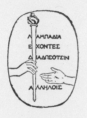

HARPER & BROTHERS PUBLISHERS
NEW YORK AND LONDON
1923

FOREIGN INFLUENCES IN
ELIZABETHAN PLAYS

FOR C. D. S.

PREFACE

It is the general purpose of this book to trace the chief foreign influences that affected the drama in England from its more regular beginnings in the reign of Henry VIII to the years immediately preceding the restoration of King Charles II. Not only are borrowings of plot and character considered, but methods of treatment, influences that concerned the varieties and kinds of English dramas, the handling of foreign historical material, national and political prejudices as affecting English plays and other like matters. The point of view is that of a student of English drama rather than that of an expert in international literature; and for this reason the reflex influences of England on the drama in other countries have been, for the most part, excluded. The demands of the subject preclude the possibility of a strict chronological treatment. The movement is necessarily that of a shuttle in the loom, now forward now backward. It is hoped that the motion may be none the less steadily onward, and that the pattern may be clearly discernible in the completed fabric.

CONTENTS

FOREIGN INFLUENCES IN ELIZABETHAN PLAYS

FOREIGN INFLUENCES IN ELIZABETHAN PLAYS

I

JONSON AND THE CLASSICS

IN attempting the discussion of such a subject as
that of foreign influences in our old English
drama, it would seem that somewhat ought to be
plead in confession and avoidance. The dignified
and mouth-filling term "comparative literature" has
always filled the writer with a certain awe and respect, if not with consternation. It may mean so
much, this laying together of the old with the new,
the ancient with the modern, the familiar with the
unfamiliar, to derive thereout a deduction novel and
startling. Or it may mean so little: a species of
small detective work by which some petty anecdote
or casual allusion is "hounded" through twenty
languages and again as many authors, to be run to
earth in the *Mahabarata*, the *Kalevala*, or ken-
neled, like a fox, in some outlandish saga, edda or
other grandmother's tale. The deadly parallel is
assuredly to be respected; but, it may be submitted,

only with the respect which we accord to anything else that is deadly. The author does not welcome it or make it too commonly a thing of his familiar handling; though he holds in a becoming regard all those who habitually have to do with such things. To speak seriously, it seems not irrational to suppose it possible for two men to have had the same idea without collusion; to hold that in the long run human nature is so to be depended on that similar causes will almost inevitably conduce to similar results. It may be suggested that the actions and interactions of literature are by no means confined to the written word, and that the subtler influences of a man's blood, his education, his sojourn in foreign parts, even his conversation and association, may often prove more potent in their effects than any reading or search for material. Perhaps to this sketch of a literary creed might be added the statement that the writer's personal studies have only been incidentally comparative. He has been no great hunter in the fields of the eternal likenesses of things, but has been content to chronicle the quarries of others in the modest role of an historian of our older drama. Much less would it become him to assume the right to speak with authority of the great dramas of the ancients, of France or of Spain. A certain young student of divinity was once asked about his studies in modern agnostic philosophy and science. He confessed in some confusion to the reading of several very advanced and radical writers but hastened to add: "Of course I read such stuff as this only for purposes of refutation." So the present author's excursions into the drama, other than that of England, have been largely for purposes of comparison, source and illustration and because he was led thither in the course of his vocation, the study of the Elizabethan age. No excuse need be made for viewing the age of that incomparable queen and her two successors from the vantage point of England, and the court will rather cite English witnesses as to things foreign than foreign witnesses as to things in England seen with alien eyes; for after all it is Englishmen and English plays as affected by things foreign with which we are concerned.

Our first topic is Ben Jonson and the influences of the classics. Obviously scholars and dramatists were interested in the classics and influenced by them long before the days of Jonson; and his name marks merely the height to which an influence continuously potent attained in an age otherwise prevalently romantic. English drama, like all other drama of western Europe, began in the Church and consisted at first in a species of illustrative amplification of the story of the bible and in the invention of other stories and allegories intended to teach right living and correct conduct and doctrine. The language of the older sacred drama was Latin, for Latin was the language of the Church. But the Latin of the Church was not the literary language of the ancients; despite the story of the German nun Hrotswitha and her attempt, in the twelfth century, to teach religion by means of Roman comedy and the not dissimilar later Christianized Terence, it is not to the sacred drama that we must look for the earliest manifestations of a direct influence of the classics in English drama. Indeed the best opinion holds that little or nothing of the literary classics was carried over to account for the impulse that begot the dramatized Scriptures of the miracle plays. The revival of the classics was the distinctive work of the renaissance; and humanism was the specific feature of the earlier spirit of the renaissance which accounts for the resuscitation of the drama of Seneca, Plautus and Terence on the modern stage.

The literary movement of the fourteenth and the two successive centuries popularly called humanism, with its revolt against scholasticism and its exaltation of the arts and the culture of the ancients, was quite as broad as the renaissance itself. With its liberality, its spirit of inquiry and its deep interest in education, humanism was sure to hit on the drama as a means to further its larger aims. Indeed the application of the drama to humanist ends was less a discovery than a transfer to these specific ends of a didactic principle that had long animated the old sacred drama. The moralities of that pugnacious and redoubtable old controversialist, Bishop Bale—best known among them, his *King Johan*—were all of them an application of the drama to the defence and inculcation of Protestant doctrine; and a similar application of the classics to the more peaceful purposes of the schoolmaster was in the spirit of the time.

Udall's *Floures of Latine Speking,* 1535, is a phrase-book made up out of comedies of Terence. And from the reading of Latin plays to the acting of them was a natural step. This step had already been taken abroad, at Rome in 1485, in Florence three years later. Terence was acted at Metz in Carnival time, Plautus at the University of Vienna, Seneca at Wittenberg with a prologue by Melancthon in 1526, the *Plutus* of Aristophanes at Zwickau, conducted by George Agricola in 1521, in Latin and Greek. The acting of classical drama soon reached England where we hear of the *Plutus* once more as performed at Christmas, 1536, at St. John's College and of a second play of Aristophanes, the *Pax,* ten years later. At Oxford both the *Menaechmi* of Plautus and the *Eunuchus* of Terence are recorded as acted at Merton, 1568. Were our topic the academic drama, which flourished at the universities and in some of the greater schools throughout the lifetime of Shakespeare and after, we might follow in the wake of Professor Boas and his excellent work on this topic.† But our concern is with classical influences on the professional drama itself, however we may glance aside from time to time at these academic parallels.

From the performance of plays of classical authors, it was but the next step to the imitation of them; and in this the pedagogic purpose found ever its place. Such was the school drama, as it has been called, of such men as Gnapheus in Holland, of Kirchmeyer in Germany, of Textor in France; and its medium was always Latin. As to the British isles, the name of George Buchanan stands first among the humanist scholars who thus attempted an application of the drama of the ancients to the purposes of education; and the circumstances of this case are interesting in themselves. The humanists not only held to Latin, the universal language of scholarship, but they prided themselves, like the Dutch Erasmus or the Spanish Vives, on being citizens of the world. Buchanan was hunted from' his native Scotland by the enmity of Cardinal Beaton and, seeking refuge, became a professor of Latin, about 1540, at the newly founded College de Guyenne at Bordeaux. It was there that he translated two of the tragedies of Euripides into Latin in accordance with a custom requiring each professor to compose an annual Latin play. To other

---

†F. S. Boas, *University Drama*, 1914.

neo-classical tragedies of Buchanan, also written
during his sojourn at Bordeaux, are on Biblical
story, the one on Jephtha, the other on John the
Baptist, in Latin and in imitation of the Euripidean
style. Among the students who took part in these
plays was Montaigne the celebrated essayist, who
records his old tutor as among the best Latin poets
of his time, as well he might.†

And now the writing of Latin plays on models
of the ancients became an established usage at the
universities, in England as well as on the continent;
and many were the learned discussions of style,
quantity, of things permitted and things not per-
missible, among such men as Ascham, tutor to the
royal children of Henry VIII, Grimald, editor of
Tottel's Miscellany, and others less known to us for
other reasons. In the very year of Buchanan's
tragedies at Bordeaux, an English schoolmaster,
John Palsgrave, worked up the *Acolastus* of
Gnapheus into a species of Latin text-book.
Acolastus was by far the most famous of the continental school dramas and begot a large progeny
there as well as in England. In subject the play is
ultimately referable to the parable of the prodigal
son, the most obvious and the most powerful example for forcing into the minds of the young the
contrasted careers of the good boy, and more es-

†*Essais,* ed. Paris, 1894, ii, 65.

pecially the bad. In 1540, Englishmen had as yet done little to suggest the great literature that was to come, and Palsgrave, in his dedication to King Henry, makes plain his position. "Not only," says he, "for I esteem that little volume to be a very curious and artificial compacted nosegay, gathered out of the most excellent and odoriferous sweet-smelling garden of the most pure Latin authors, but also because the maker thereof—as far as I can learn—is yet living, whereby I would be glad to move into the hearts of your Grace's clerks some little grain of honest and virtuous envy."†

This "honest and virtuous envy" soon produced adaptations of foreign plays to English conditions and, besides Latin comedies, comedies in the vernacular tongue. Such were *The Nice Wanton, The Disobedient Child* and *Misogonus* in all of which the careers of naughtiness and virtue are contrasted by the devices of situations which show an acquaintance at least with classical comedy. The culmination of these plays was reached in 1575 in George Gascoigne's *Glass of Government* wherein a Christian moral, Roman situations and the life of students at a modern university combine to depict with elaboration the contrasted careers of four youths, two of them dreary models of impeccable virtue, the others precious scamps, well deserving the

---

† *Joannis Palsgravii Londoniensis Ecphrasis Anglica in Comoediam Acolasti,* 1540, p. 7.

8

condign punishment which overtakes them. This comedy is excellently planned and written, and its courtier author, who was something of a scapegrace on his own account, succeeded, as well as many a grave "pulpiter," in giving that sprightly glamor to vice and that solemn gloom to virtue which is unhappily only too true to life.

Thus far, save for the direct imitation of Euripides in the tragedy of Buchanan, classical influences had been mainly indirect. Greek influences remained such thereafter. The influences of the Latin drama sifted down to two definite authors: Plautus for comedy, Seneca for tragedy. A brief digression concerning them will not be out of place here. Plautus belongs to an early period of the Roman stage and is, take him all in all, not much more than a translator and adapter of earlier Greek comedies to the coarser but more vigorous conditions of Roman life. His liveliness and inventive faculty, like his vigorous style, fell in well with the boisterous taste of Tudor days; hence the preference given to Plautus over the more correct and elegant, but far less original, Terence. There is scarcely one of the twenty extant plays of Plautus that is not held under requisition somewhere in Elizabethan drama for whole plots or parts thereof, and several types of Plautine character are carried over bodily into English comedy to subsist down to very late times. If Plautus was early, Seneca was correspondingly late in the history of Roman literature; there is in point of fact some two hundred and fifty years between them, years in which the "golden" literature of republican Rome had arisen, flourished and waned, to be superseded by the "silver age" of the early Caesars, falling away in the time of Nero into periods of baser metal. Eight tragedies of Seneca remain extant (the Elizabethans counted ten); and all are referable in subject to the infinitely greater Greek tragedies of Sophocles and Euripides. The salient characteristics of Seneca are correctness of style, amounting in metre to absolute rigor, a florid rhetoric and wordiness, conveying no great depth of thought but a considerable show of it. As dramas the Senecan plays are well constructed, the personages are not conspicuously realized, but horror, blood and terror take the place of the Greek reserve and dialectical argument, and discussion the place, for the most part, of the Greek poetic delineation of human passion and emotion. In a word, Seneca gives us Greek tragedy, vulgarized and modernized. Its modernity and freedom from restraint especially appealed to the Elizabethans. Lastly, of Senecan tragedy it is to be remembered that these Roman plays were not written to be acted, but to be read and declaimed, a point which adds to their artificiality and accounts for some of their defects.

It is with the very first regular English dramas that these two Roman influences become manifest

in their completeness; and these models had much
to do with the term "regular" and with the purely
imaginary line that we still draw between plays
"digested into acts," as the old phase went, and
those in which these accidental divisions are not
formally defined. The first three regular English
dramas, as everybody knows, are *Ralph Roister
Doister,* acted first somewhere between 1534 and
1541, *Gammer Gurton's Needle,* 1552-53, and
Gorboduc the first performance of which took place
before the queen on "Newyears day at night," 1562.
Grammer Gurton is vernacular English farce, however the work of a Master of Arts and acted at
Cambridge. It does not here concern us. *Roister
Doister* is a free adaptation to English scene and
conditions of the *Miles Gloriosus* of Plautus; *Gorboduc* is a tragedy on English mythical history,
conducted in the style and written in imitation of
the manner of Seneca. However, nothing could be
more misleading than to assume that these were
occasional or sporadic examples. The Latin comedies of both Plautus and Terence had long been
customarily performed by boys of the schools, such
as Eton and Westminster, on holidays and at what
we call commencements. The practise was justified
by the confidence it gave the lads in speaking and the
benefits that accrued to their Latin enunciation.
Nicholas Udall, the author of the comedy *Ralph
Roister Doister,* was a schoolmaster by profession;

11

he had been headmaster at different times of both
Eton and Westminster, and a pretty little debate as
to the date of his comedy turns on whether it was
written at one or the other school.† What Udall
really did was to substitute an English play for a
Latin one; and we know that the substitution was
immediately acclaimed, accepted and largely followed in the schools and colleges thereafter. The
case of *Gorboduc* is somewhat different. This
tragedy was the work of two young gentlemen,
Sackville and Norton, students of the Inner Temple,
one of the four societies of London devoted to the
study of the law, and their choice of an English
story in place of a classical one was as novel as
their employment of blank verse, for the first time
in a drama. But they, too, had before them preced-
ent and example. Already the year before, Jasper
Heywood, son of the famous epigrammatist, and
writer of interludes, John Heywood, had published
Seneca's *Troas* in an English translation; and the
work went on in the hands of other translators to
be completed in 1581 with the publication of a volume entitled *Seneca his Tenne Tragedies*. The
sixties, seventies and eighties are the Senecan dec-
ades and tragedies of the type flourished at court in
the universities, the inns of court, and in the schools.
Thus Gascoigne's *Jocasta*, 1566, is almost a pure

†See C. G. Child's ed. of this comedy, pp. 31-42.

translation of an Italian Senecan play; Legge's
Richardus Tertius, 1579,† returns to the Latin
tongue, preserves the Senecan manner, but takes
English historical annals for a subject; and Thomas
Hughes, *Misfortunes of Arthur,* 1587, goes back to
English and the mythical British chronicles; whilst
Tancred and Gismund deals with an Italian
story of love and revenge. Choruses, dumb shows,
to eke out their want of action, ghosts crying vengeance, soliloques, word encounters bandied phrase by
phrase, all these things are characteristic of the
early English Senecan craze; and so too are com-
monplaces of sentiment loftily expressed, obvious
moralisms delivered like Delphic oracles, a style
stiff with the embroidery of classical names and allusions, and a general air of fatalistic and lugu-
brious complaint. It is thus that Gorboduc cries
out in his woes:

O cruel Fate, O mindful wrath of gods!
Whose vengeance neither Simois stained streams
Flowing with blood of Trojan princes slain,
Nor Phrygian fields made rank with corpses dead
Of Asian kings and lords, can yet appease;
Nor slaughter of unhappy Priam's race,
Nor Ilions fall made level with the soil,
Can yet suffice; but still-continued rage
Pursues our lives, and from the farthest seas

---

†See the interesting account of this Latin play by Boas,
as above, p. 112 ff.

Doth chase the issues of destroyed Troy.
"Oh, no man happy till his end be seen,"
If any flowing wealth and seeming joy
In present years might make a happy wight,
Happy was Hecuba, the wofullest wretch
That ever lived to make a mirror of;
And happy Priam with his noble sons;
And happy I, till now, alas, I see
And feel my most unhappy wretchedness!

This is Seneca in milder mood; in his extremes, as for example in the tragedy of *Locrine,* all these characteristics are exaggerated to a degree of bombast that often becomes absurd. Classical allusion is worked to death, rage and horror overdone and big astounding terms usurp the place of ordinary speech.‡ No wonder that the wits began to exclaim at this sort of thing, to ridicule its bombast, its unreality and grandiloquence, declaring, as did Nash, that "Seneca let blood line by line and page by page at length must needs die to our stage";† whilst on the other hand Robert Wilmot, conservative Templer and confirmed Senecan, "conjured" his drama *Tancred and Gismund,* revived as late as 1591, that she be not so proud of her fresh painting "to straggle in her plumes abroad, but to confine herself within the walls of your house [that is the

‡*Gorboduc,* iii, 1; and *Locrine,* especially, "Reprint of the Malone Society," lines 1308-1330.
†*Menaphon,* "To the Gentlemen Students, 1589, Grosart, *Greene,* vi. 15.

Inner Temple]; so am I sure she shall be safe from the tragedian tyrants of our time."†

But "the tragedian tyrants" had already seized upon Seneca and haled him, ghosts, bombast, classical gods and all, onto the boards of the popular stage, there to astonish the citizens of London for a decade longer and enter ·into many a tragedy of fame that even now we read with admiration. The process of this transfer of Seneca, translated and imitated by the scholars and gentlemen of the Inns of Court, to Seneca imitated and popularized for the public stage is not known in its precise terms. But it seems not unlikely that the transfer was made through some such person as George Peele, one of those men of ready and adaptable talent who made way in his plays and poems for the greater genius of Shakespeare. Peele, when at Oxford, appears to have been associated with his kinsman, William Gager, in the acting, revising and staging of Latin plays, for which Gager enjoyed an enviable contemporary reputation. Thence Peele transferred his talents to the court and, early in the eighties, perhaps preceded Lyly—the accepted dramatist of the court, and an admirable adapter of Plautus, witness his *Mother Bombie*—in plays of graceful poetic type, adapting classical stories more or less to con-

---

†"To the Gentlemen of the Temple," the Malone Society's reprint of this play.

temporary court life.† Such a play is Peele's *Arraignment of Paris* which is absolutely devoid of influences either Plautine or Senecan; but it reproduces, by means of exquisite poetry, a charming myth of ancient times in a manner comparable to the contemporary decorative paintings that employed the stories of gods and heroes to adorn the halls of kings and the boudoirs of princesses. But Peele did not long flourish at court. He had neither wealth, birth, temperance nor patience to support him; and drifting to the town he soon became active as a writer for the popular stage, trying his hand at every variety of drama then in vogue to support a Bohemian if not a dissolute existence. Into the intricacies of his career we need not pry. It is not certain that he is the author of the tragedy entitled *Locrine,* on the stage we may well believe by about 1585; but, whether so or not, here is Seneca, bombast, grandiloquence, solemn declamation and an overplus of sonorous classical names, all present, popularized by means of interlarded comic action and the more active melodrama that has ever its unmistakeable appeal to the masses.

The immediate times produced a greater man than Peele in whom popularized Seneca reached its height. Thomas Kyd is memorable as the author of *The Spanish Tragedy,* the first vital tragedy in

---

†On the relations of Peele and Lyly, see A. Feuillerat, *John Lyly*, 1910.

our language and one which divided with Marlowe's *Tamburlaine* a popularity that surpassed all plays outside of Shakespeare until the years of the close of Elizabeth's reign. *The Spanish Tragedy* must soon have followed *Locrine*. It was seasoned by two or three years on the stage when the Armada came to stir England to a frenzy against Spain and the Pope. In subject Kyd's masterpiece is a tragedy of revenge, the revenge of a father for the murder of his son, slain under circumstances that at first defy discovery and, later, redress by ordinary means. The Senecan features of *The Spanish Tragedy* are many. The play opens like the *Thyestes* with Ghost and Revenge, and the chorus and dumb shows (the latter an English Senecan feature) are maintained; Senecan conventions of speech, rhetoric and classical allusion recur; and in places whole passages are translated from the Roman tragedian. On the other hand the original of the story of *The Spanish Tragedy* has been sought for in vain and its scenes are pervaded with a spirit of independence, originality and with a romantic atmosphere such as was new to the English stage.

It was no less a man than Ben Jonson, years after on one of the later revivals of the play, who furnished certain "additions" by means of which the protagonist, the old Marshal Hieronimo, was more vitally portrayed. The subject of these "additions" is an interesting one, but it scarcely con-

cerns our account of the growth and assimilation of
the influences of Seneca on the tragedy of Elizabeth's age. As a matter of fact it is not in these
"additions" that Jonson is classical; his classicality
is wider and based upon sounder foundations than
the accidental choice of a single dramatic author as
a model for a single play. Indeed it may be
affirmed that Seneca and Plautus became the examples which they were to English drama merely
from the circumstance that they were really the only
available models. In thought, style, manner and
imagery and non-dramatic authors of ancient Rome
wielded an influence far wider than the drama, and
classical quotation, translation, imitation and inspiration were universally the order of the hour.
Indeed, when Elizabeth first came to the throne,
there was little to read save the classics. In the
well known words of Macaulay: "The Italian was
the only modern language which possessed anything
that could be called a literature. All the valuable
books then extant in all the vernacular dialects of
Europe would hardly have filled a single shelf.
England did not yet possess Shakespeare's plays,
and *The Faery Queen,* nor France Montaigne's
Essays nor Spain *Don Quixote* * * * Chaucer,
Gower, Froissart, Comines, Rabelais, nearly complete the list."† Necessarily men read and were

---

†"Lord Bacon," *Works of Macaulay, Essays,* American ed.
1860, iii, 350.

educated by the classics and learned to think in terms of Plato and Aristotle as they learned to write on the precepts and examples of Quintilian and Cicero. Nor does it in any wise imperil the truth of this statement that many of these classical ideas came to England through the sieve of Italian or French criticism. The point lies in that the ultimate authority was that of the ancients, as Ascham, Elizabeth's tutor, put it: "As for the Latin or Greek tongue, everything is so excellently done in them, that none can do better. In the English tongue, contrary, everything in a manner so meanly, both for the matter and handling, that no man can do worse. * * * They which had least hope in Latin have been most bold in English."† But this day was soon coming to its close.

Let us turn now to Ben Jonson in whom above all other men of his time centered the classical ideal in its application to English conditions. Ten years the junior of Marlowe and Shakespeare, despite poverty and untoward conditions, Jonson became, even in young manhood, one of the most classically learned men among his contemporaries, holding the ancients, as it has been happily put, in solution in his ample mind to use at will, as free from the suspicion of plagiarism as he was above the awkwardness of pedantry. Jonson's classicism was alto-

---

†Ascham, *Toxophilus*, ed. Arber, 1868, p. 18.

gether different from the empirical classicism of men like Sidney and Barnes who experimented with Greek and Roman measures in English lyrical poetry; and it was above the reach of the early imitators and borrowers from Seneca and Plautus. Jonson's grasp, understanding and easy use of the ideas, the technical practices, the style and subject matter of ancient authors may be called an assimilated classicism; and no one approached him in these qualities in his time except George Chapman, the famous translator of Homer, whose comedies in the Plautine manner are among the most diverting of our old dramas. Possessed of this assimilated knowledge of ancient literature it may be said of Jonson that he is less a borrower of plots than an expander of suggestions, less an imitator of single personages or situations than an adapter of what was most available to the purposes of his English comedies. Still, persons, plots and situations in Jonson's comedies are often directly inspired by the classics. For example in *Every Man in His Humor,* Captain Bobadil is as palpably the braggart Pyrgopolinices of the *Miles Gloriosus* of Plautus as Brainworm is the ubiquitous clever servant of Roman comedy; Jonson's *Case is Altered* combines situations from the *Captivi* of Plautus with parts of the *Aulularia,* as the *Alchemist* has been traced in parts to the *Mostellaria* and the *Poenulus.* Save for the *Alchemist* these examples are from earlier plays.

Jonson's more usual method was the expansion of a hint. Thus the droll suggestion of a wretched husband, so maddened by the eternal chatter of a talkative wife that he appears before the judges to gain their permission to drink hemlock and die, Jonson worked up from the Sophist Labanius into the inventive and amusing plot of *The Silent Woman.* The resolution of the difficulty in this case, a mock wedding ending in the discovery that the supposed wife is a boy, Jonson owes to his recollection of such a device in the *Casina* of Plautus. In the same comedy of Jonson may be found a bit of dialogue modelled on the *Ars Amatoria* of Ovid, its sweetness curdled in the process by the acrid humor of the English satirist; in *Poetaster* the greater part of one of the satires of Horace has been dramatized with admirable effect and the climax of the play, the trial of the poets, derives direct from Aristophanes. More important than these things—than the translation of an oration of Cicero in *Sejanus* or the borrowing of an episode from Lucan—is the whole pose of Jonson as a dramatic satirist, a pose the sublime assurance and arrogance of which is derived directly from the Roman satirist, Juvenal, whose bitterness, causticity and amazing command of invective Jonson admired above the qualities of all ancient authors. Jonson's whole theory of the drama, like his theory of life, was based on this study and assimilation of the ancients; and, had it

21

not been for the essentially sturdy and practical nature of his English fibre at heart, he might easily have been transmuted into the supine and slavish follower of outworn classical forms and usages which the ignorance of those whose scholarship habitually follows my leader has been sometimes misled into representing him.

As the Jonsonian theories and practices are an important gift of the classics to our English drama, let us go into both of them somewhat. When about 1596 Jonson began to write comedies there were, roughly speaking, three schools of comedy in vogue, that which was purely vernacular, as yet only rudely represented (unless we except the scenes of English life in the comedies of Greene), secondly the romantic comedy of Italy (as exampled say in *The Two Gentlemen of Verona*), and thirdly Anglicized Plautus, (despite some clever Italianate examples at court) best seen in Shakespeare's successful experiment, *The Comedy of Errors*. This comedy, it will be remembered, doubles the difficulties of resemblance as represented in the *Menaechmi* of Plautus, its source. It is noticeable that Shakespeare, despite this success, never returned to the comedy of Plautus, though the motive of mistaken identity through similarity of person and dress recurs in *Twelfth Night* and elsewhere. Shakespeare's nature was romantic, his touch with the classics was momentary and we have reason to believe that it was indirect. Jonson's experiment, which contrasts with Shakespeare's *Comedy of Errors,* is *The Case is Altered* in which, though he borrows direct from Plautus, he attempts romantic comedy. Jonson never acknowledged nor republished this play, but reverted at once to classical ideals in *Every Man in his Humor,* 1598, in which he first set forth his theory of humors, a theory which comports entirely with the Aristotelian idea of comedy and with the practices of Aristophanes and the Roman comedians.

A "humor" to Jonson was a warp in character, a bias of disposition by which

> Some one peculiar quality
> Doth so affect a man that it doth draw
> All his effects, his spirits, and his powers
> In their confluctions, all to run one way.†

In comedy, so conceived, character is exalted above incident and complexity in disposition is reduced to the common denominator of some ruling trait. Brainworm's passion for gulling or fooling everybody, Bobadil's imaginative boastfulness and cowardice, Morose's abhorrence of noise, Mammon's greed for gold and itch to be a grandee—these things are Jonsonian "humorous" personages; and Jonson deprecated the idea of some triviality of

---

†*Every Man Out of His Humor,* Induction, ed. Cunningham-Gifford, 1871-75, ii, 16.

dress, some accidental mannerism of speech or the
like as in any wise constituting a true "humor."
To this conception of character, to which he literally adhered throughout his life, Jonson added a
nicety and ingeniousness in dramatic construction
which he derived likewise from the ancients. Jonson is the most consummate dramatist constructively
of his age. It may be doubted if in actual ingenuity of construction he has ever been surpassed. Like
all the classicists, Jonson had an innate respect for
those three fates or furies, known and venerated as
the three unities. But these important personages
demand a paragraph to themselves.

The three graces of dramatic classicality are the
unities of time, place and action: they became far
more than graces, notably in classical France, and
were worshipped as a trinity and quite as little
understood. Romantic drama in this matter has
always been of the Arian or Soccinian heresy and
worshipped but one unity in constructive drama,
and that is unity of action. Of late even that faith
has gone by the board and we are become, at least
at times, sad agnostics and unbelievers. Jonson
however was no idolater although he believed that
it was well, if possible, to limit the action of a play
to as short a time as possible, to make that time
continuous and to avoid changes of scene. For
example he would have reprobated the change of
scene from Alexandria to Rome, from Rome to

Actium and back to Alexandria of Shakespeare's *Antony and Cleopatra.* There are nine or ten changes of locality in the fifteen scenes of the fourth act of this play. Jonson would likewise have reprobated the lapse of sixteen years which Time, as chorus, asks us to forgive between the third and fourth acts of *The Winter's Tale* in order that Perdita may grow up to be a marriageable young woman the while. Does the reader's dramatic Soccinianism allow him to approve these things? And yet, speaking of ancient freedom in these and other particulars, Jonson does not hesitate to say: "I see not, then, but we should enjoy the same licence, or free power to illustrate and heighten our inventions, as they did; and not be tied to those strict and regular forms which the niceness of a few, who are nothing but form, would thrust upon us."†

It was in the interests of dramatic clarity that Jonson sought a simplification of the complexities of human nature, a common denominator for the diversity of mankind. This he thought that he had found in the presentation of certain types referable ultimately, in his moralist's and satirist's conception of life, to two classes of men, the fools and the knaves. And it was only his abundant wit and inventive resourcefulness that succeeded in keeping

---

†*Ibid*, p. 23.

such personages human and interesting. Jonson's reasonable and restrictive art was precisely what was needed in his day by way of example to check and somewhat rein in the wild and splendid career of the glorious horses of romance. His function was that of a conservative criticism, notwithstanding that he has left little formal comment, as such, on the art of his time.

Turning to Jonson's tragedies, these are two in number, *Sejanus*, 1603, and *Catiline his Conspiracy*, 1611. The first is a consummate study in classical portraiture and written, it would seem not unlikely, in deliberate emulation of the success of Shakespeare's *Julius Caesar; Catiline* is the final expression of Jonson's theories as to English tragedy. It is not to be imputed to unrighteousness in Shakespeare, that whatever he touched in the drama he rendered into the terms of contemporary Elizabethan life. It is not only that King John, Macbeth, King Lear or Coriolanus, the Elizabethan doublet impartially covers them all, but the thoughts and ideals, the sentiments and conduct of Shakespeare's personages are Tudor and Stuart. That life was large and much in it remains as significant today as when it was written. But the discontent of Mr. Shaw with Shakespeare and the trammels which his art has riveted on modern drama is not unjustified nor unfounded. Jonson alone among his contemporaries seems to have possessed the historical sense that realizes a past age in its own likeness. He alone was sensitive to such things as the sombreroes of the conspirators and the striking clock in *Julius Caesar*, the pistol used against Pericles, Cleopatra's game of billiards, or that geographical aberration, "the seacoast of Bohemia." Shakespeare's classical material, it is well known, came to him by devious courses and his chief authority for Roman history was North's *Plutarch*, the English translation of a French translation of a Latin translation of a Greek biographer who chronicled Caesar, to him a foreigner, nearly a hundred and fifty years after Caesar's death. When Jonson studied history he wanted to get nearer to the facts. Accordingly in *Sejanus* Jonson went to the immediate authorities, Tacitus and Suetonius in particular, and penned his play in protest against the want of perspective, the carelessness as to historical accuracy which characterized the handling of classical subjects on the stage. Only the pedantry that tempted him to refer in footnotes to his authorities has turned the less discerning from a due appreciation of the success with which Jonson has transferred in this tragedy the subtle and enigmatic features of the Tiberius of Tacitus to scenes instinct with the very life of imperial Rome. The heroic stoicism of Brutus, the sharp acquisitiveness of Cassius; Antony, careless and pleasure-loving, yet master of a natural eloquence that raised to mutiny the stones of

Rome,—these are men drawn to the life as Jonson could never have drawn them. But if the scholarly reader would see ancient Rome, her "very form and pressure," hear such speech as Romans might have uttered, and see the life of forum, atrium and senate chamber, let him turn to *Sejanus* and to *Catiline,* not to *Caesar* or *Coriolanus.*

Jonson drew the materials for his *Catiline* from Sallust and Cicero, following them with a scholar's faithfulness and continuing to reproduce from his knowledge of the satirists as well as the historians a vivid picture of the social life of ancient Rome. The scenes in which figure the fickle, wanton Fulvia and Sempronia, vain of her knowledge of Greek and ambitious to be dabbling in politics, are second to nothing in the satirical high comedy that the age has left us. *Catiline,* as compared with *Sejanus* displays a retrogression to earlier ideals and a stricter observance of the minor practices if not of the larger spirit of Seneca. Thus the drama opens with an Induction in which figures the ghost of Sylla; and lyrical choruses in a variety of metres interlard the acts. But these Roman plays of Jonson are no mere Senecan tragedies, they have risen to heights beyond the attainments of a merely imitative age, and the qualified repute in which they are held by critics who write of Jonson and his time is referable to the inevitable contrast which they invite with the work of the greatest romantic genius that the world has yet known. The sun obscures the brightest stars by day and it is only when our eyes are not dazzled with the blaze of romantic art that we can enjoy the calm serenity of the classic age. There are many stars in that deep, cool sky; among those late to rise and caught and dimmed in the glory of romantic sunshine was Ben Jonson.

And now as to Shakespeare, his knowledge or ignorance of the classics has been the subject of scholarly disquisition from the days of Farmer's celebrated essay on the learning of Shakespeare, way back in 1776, to the late Mr. Churton Collins and his admirable discussion, some few years since, on Shakespeare as a Classical Scholar. It was Jonson who declared in print that Shakespeare had "small Latin and less Greek." And this dictum has rung down the ages, closing the ponderous gates of the humanities on Shakespeare and leaving him without in the dreary land of Philistia. But John Aubrey, that delightful old gossip of the cavalier generation, declared that Shakespeare "knew Latin pretty well." Reports concerning a man's acquaintance with any foreign tongue are apt to depend on the ignorance or on the knowledge of the person making the report. Admiring ignorance exaggerates knowledge in others; knowledge belittles less knowledge. The truth of the matter in this case of Shakespeare appears to lie somewhere between the two extremes, and his knowledge of the classics was as worthy of the admiration of Aubrey who was little lettered, as it was deserving of the deprecatory words of the learned Jonson. But Collins claimed more: that Shakespeare could "read Latin with as much facility as a cultivated Englishman of our own time reads French; that with some at least of the principal Latin classics he was intimately acquainted; that through the Latin language he had access to the Greek classics; and that of the Greek classics in Latin versions he had in all probability a remarkably extensive knowledge."†

Most students of Shakespeare will be surprised at claims so large—and they are, one cannot but think, excessive,—including as they do the satires of Horace, Juvenal and Persius, the narrative poetry of Ovid, the philosophy of Lucretius, the lyrics of the Greek anthology in Latin, the dramatic theory of Aristotle and the dramatic practice of Seneca and Plautus, besides reminiscence and parallel, especially in Greek tragedy, altogether surprising when gathered together and pressed home. It may be suggested, however, that likenesses in psychology, such in particular as that between Clytemnestra and Lady Macbeth, between Alcestis

---

†"Shakespeare as a Classical Scholar", *Studies in Shakespeare*, 1904, pp. 3, 4. More recent contributions on this topic are P. J. Enk, *Neophilologus*, 1920, p. 359 ff, and R. S. Conway, *New Studies in a Great Inheritance*, 1921, discusses somewhat unsatisfactorily the influence of Vergil in *The Tempest*.

and Katherine the shrew, for example, are really tributes to the accuracy of the observation of the Greek and the English poet in like situations rather than suggestions, much less proofs, of contact between the two minds. In an examination of many an alleged parallel in scene, personage or name, the usual result is the finding, sooner or later, of an English intermediary. The names "Tranio" and "Grumio" in *The Taming of the Shrew,* for example, and more especially the laughable scene with the pedant, are certainly referable to Plautine comedy. But Shakespeare had them all, beyond the peradventure of a doubt, from *The Taming of a Shrew* and Gascoigne's *Supposes,* the two old English comedies on which the Shakespearean revision was founded. Again, when we hear that William Warner had made "diverse versions of Plautus' comedies * * * Englished for the use and delight of his private friends, who in Plautus' own words are not able to understand them", it is more reasonable to assume that Shakespeare was one of these "private friends" or the borrower of a book from him, than to attribute to Shakespeare, on lack of definite proof of this last, a direct borrowing from the Latin text. Once more, when we find the subject of *Twelfth Night* in two Italian plays and in a Latin version entitled *Laelia,* acted at Cambridge in 1590 as well, it is obvious that Shakespeare might have seen this last, but with a fourth, quite sufficient

31

source, in Bartholomew Riche's story of *Apolonius and Silla* in English which sufficiently supplies all the events of *Twelfth Night*, it is obviously as unnecessary, as it is inept, to seek a source which involves a knowledge either of Latin or Italian, for this play. Shakespeare may have known both languages, but his use of a source for *Twelfth Night* proves nothing on this score.‡ Lastly, on this topic, it is notable that Professor Cunliffe in examining the Senecan influences on Shakespeare declared, some years since, that Shakespeare's knowledge of the original text of Seneca must turn on his authorship of *Titus Andronicus*, the play of all the most dubiously his.† It will be the task of the next writer on the learning of Shakespeare to attack the fabric that Collins reared and he will have to be furnished with considerable classical amunition to demolish its outworks, though many of them no doubt are certain of ultimate demolition. Leaving this work of destruction to the future, we may none the less express the conviction that, living in an age when everybody read Latin, Shakespeare probably read that classic tongue at least as well as a modern American college senior; he was doubtless not quite so proud of his accomplishment, as it was then not

---

‡On the relation of these plays, see Boas, *University Drama*, p. 296 ff.

†J. W. Cunliffe, *The Influence of Seneca on Elizabethan Tragedy*, 1893.

so unusual. So we may infer in conclusion of the subject of Shakespeare's knowledge of the classics that Bagehot underrates his Latin when he declares it much like that of the Eton boy of whom it was said that it was not so much knowledge as an acquaintance with the hard fact that there actually are such languages as Latin and Greek and that the less a decent boy has to do with them the better. Shakespeare knew more of Latin at least than this; perhaps, after all, it was not much more.

When we think of the kinship of the expanding Elizabethan mind with that of the Athens of Pericles, it seems somewhat remarkable that the dramatists were so little affected by the great literature of Greece. Homer, Hesiod, Theocritus, Musaeus and Heliodorus, all were translated in whole or in part during the age; there appears to have been no complete translation of Aeschylus, Sophocles, Euripides or Aristophanes, all of whom, it may be suspected, were known chiefly in Latin translations. It may be affirmed, then, that Greek tragedy is not to be accounted among the palpable influences affecting English drama in the times of Elizabeth and James, save so far as Euripides may be allowed to have filtered through the very coarse sacking of Seneca. Save for Jonson, Aristophanes is as absent in effect, and Terence, so far as representative of earlier Greek comedy, though several of his plays are translated, yields to the wider, spright-

lier spirit of the more wholly Latin Plautus. Aside
from borrowings of plots, situations, characters, and
the translation and imitation of passages and sentiments, the influence of Roman tragedy and comedy
on our old drama was chiefly regulative. The idea
of structure, of division into acts and scenes, pro-
logues and other extraneous parts of the play, the
soliloquy, the aside, *stichomythia*, the hard term
for the serious banter of words in like verse structure, and many more of these minor things are referable to the example of classical drama; and the
Elizabethan ghost, like several of his more fleshly
embodied fellows in comedy and tragedy, takes his
descent from the same august source. But outside
of Jonson, and perhaps Chapman, the popular dramatists were little selective in the choice of their
sources for classical subjects; and more often than
not the dilution through mediaeval versions and
perversions resulted in strange romantic distortions.
Among these none is more remarkable than Shakespeare's *Troilus and Cressida,* for example, which
harks back to Chaucer and Caxton's *Recuyell of the
Histories of Troy* with a likely intervention of some
English drama or more on the way. The idea that
Shakespeare, in some of the bitter and trivial scenes
of this play, is satirizing antiquity is not borne out
by a closer acquaintance with his sources. Medieval
art translated everything with the most child-like
frankness into the terms of its own ideals and un-

derstanding; and none the least of its charm is the circumstance that, outside of a few classicists, Elizabethan literature, too, did very much the same. This powerful and unmistakably Shakespearean drama of Troilus and his Cressida may necessitate in the reader, who comes to it for a first time, a revision of his generalizations as to its great author; but the making of him a closer student of antiquity will not be among them.†

These are only some of the larger lines of classical influence on our old English drama. Among the greater writers for the popular stage few there were who did not at some time touch upon classical subjects. Lodge, charming lyrist and author of the dainty pastoral romance whence Shakespeare had the story of his *As You Like It,* also wrote a somewhat dreary tragedy on the wars of Marius and Sulla. Nash, the trenchant satirist and master of billigsgate, collaborated with Marlowe in dramatizing the story of Æneas and Dido. Marston worked up a favorite continental theme, Sophonisba; and Webster, that of Appius and Virginia. As to ready, popular, busy Thomas Heywood, besides a perfunctory treatment in drama of the unhappy fate

---

†See on this topic, J. S. P. Tatlock, *The Chief Problem in Shakespeare,* "Sewanee Review," 1916; the same writer's, *Siege of Troy in Elizabethan Literature.* "Modern Language Review," 1915; and the valuable essay of Sir W. Raleigh, ed. of *Shakespeare,* "Jefferson Press," 1908, vol. xvi.

of Lucrece, spoiled by an incredible intrusion of comic ribaldry into its scenes, he literally dramatized the mythology of Ovid's *Metamorphoses* in a series of rambling plays, omitting little and extenuating less. The siege of Troy, too, forms the subject of no less than two of Heywood's ready and capable plays. Popularization of the classics could go no further. The greater heroes of antiquity recur again and again on the Elizabethan stage. Not to mention Alexander, Cyrus, Xerxes, Antiochus and even Hannibal, the story of Julius Caesar was acted two years before the birth of Shakespeare, and there are some half a dozen other plays on the great Roman before Shakespeare came to write on the theme. There are three old plays on Nero, as many more involving Cleopatra, besides Shakespeare's *Antony and Cleopatra;* and at least one other Troilus and Timon. In comedy, Heywood, Marston, Dekker, Chapman, Fletcher, Ford and Shirley use material derived from a great variety of classical sources. At the universities of Oxford and Cambridge, Seneca imitated and Plautus revised continued in steady repetition throughout the age, precisely as if Shakespeare and the romantic drama had never existed. If we add to this, the indirect influence of the classics in their ideals of restraint, in conception of character, style and all the rest, as passed on to future times through the intervention of the score of Jonson's imitators, we can not but appreciate the degree of influence which Latin literature exerted on the drama of the time. In a word Elizabeth's time and that of James were far better read in the classics than are we and infinitely more directly affected by them; and it was Jonson who was the lens through which these influences of classical literature were chiefly refracted, so far at least as they illuminated the stage.

II

SHAKESPEARE AND THE LURE OF ITALY

ITALY, to the Tudor imagination, was the golden land of romance. It was there that the poets lived, the painters and the famous mechanicians in printing, architecture, statuary and war. It was there that learned writers on art, philosophy, statecraft and civil life set a standard of culture and conduct for the civilized world, penning works that were to inure through the ages. In Italy had happened much in fact and story: Rome and Roman grandeur, the pomp and all-spreading power of the universal Church, mediaeval tales of passion, crime, devotion, patriotism. What was there that had not come to Italy or out of her? There had once lived the Trojan Æneas, founder of the Roman race, through Brutus, progenitor of Britain, which took its name from him. The great Julius Caesar had come from Rome to conquer the British Isles; King Arthur had gone from Britain to conquer Rome: both stories were equally credible. In Italy had once dwelt Vergil, to the mediaeval imagination a necromancer, learned in the forbidden sciences, astrology that foretells the things to come, witchcraft that adds the aid of familiar spirits and devils to man in the pursuit of his desires, alchemy that solves the secrets of life and death, and makes man all powerful with the philosopher's stone. Moreover in Italy had lived long ago that wicked Circe, turning rational men to loathsome beasts and swine by the allurements of her beauty and the enchantments of her fatal wiles.

But the Tudor mind, which was as rational as it was imaginative, knew the Italy of its own time with a more actual acquaintance than this. Passing such belated mediaeval travellers as Guylforde, in 1506, and Torkington not long after, William Thomas, as early as 1549, described Italy with admirable discernment, antiquarian and political; and Sir Thomas Hoby, type of the gentleman traveller, besides a private diary giving his impressions of court life in Italy, not yet printed, translated in 1561, his excellent version of Castiglione's *Courtier,* which became the example not only in general of courtly behavior and conduct, but the model for many like books in the English tongue. It is Thomas who informs us that the English gentlemen that he met in almost every Italian city "resort hither principally under pretence of study"; and it was that "pretence" that Ascham reprobated in his *Scholemaster,* declaring that he knew many who had "returned out of Italy worse transformed than were ever any in Circe's court." Later literature is full of warnings against the allurements, the vices and the deadly crimes of that beautiful land. "O Italy!" says Nash, "academy of manslaughter, the sporting place of murder, the apothecary shop of all nations! How many kinds of weapons hast thou invented for malice!" And Gascoigne enjoins a friend about to travel thither to "beware of poison when invited to dinners, never to drink before another had tasted the beverage, to be on the outlook for poisoned soap and take care lest the tailor stuff his doublet with what might bring on a deadly sweat."† None the less to Italy said Dallington, "all nations of Christendom do flock"; and conversely from Italy the learning, the arts and especially the statecraft of the renaissance was radiated throughout Europe. As to England, it was in the reign of King Henry VIII that these influences were first felt to the full. Vives, a Spaniard, might lecture for a time at Oxford and cosmopolitan Erasmus naturalize himself an Englishman; but the king's master of ceremonies, his foreign secretaries, his artists, musicians, and actors were Italians all, as was the architect of his father's tomb and the chief historian of his father's reign. Wolsey affected the state of an Italian cardinal, Thomas Cromwell brought the statecraft of Macchiavelli's *Prince* to bear on English politics, and Sir Thomas More translated the life of Pico della Mirandola into English that it might shine an example to Englishmen. Men modeled their conversation and their

---

† Quoted by Einstein, *Italian Renaissance in England*, 1902, p. 160.

conduct on the precepts of Guazzo or Castiglione, as they were later to quarrel and duel by the books of Grassi and Saviolo. In the days of Elizabeth few English courtiers or men of distinction were unable to speak Italian. The queen herself was an admirable linguist, and on one occasion at least the entire English counsel carried on a negotiation with the Venetian ambassador in his native tongue.

If we turn to our sphere, that of literature, Italian influences in the age of Elizabeth are best studied for the outset in those two remarkable and contrasted volumes, *The Prince* of Niccolo Macchiavelli and *The Courtier* of Baldassare Castiglione. *The Prince* curiously enough seems not to have been translated into English during the lifetime of Elizabeth, nor indeed until long after; but its influence on political ideals and diplomacy was felt throughout the age, more especially in the popular misconception made current by his French critic Gentillet, that made its frank, clear-headed, cynical and philosophical author the patron of political immorality, subterfuge, deceit and efficient lying.† It is Macchiavelli who speaks the prologue to Marlowe's *Jew of Malta,* therein declaring:

---

†See Innocent Gentillet, *Discourse sur les moyen de bien gouverner . . un royaume . . contra N. M.,* 1576; translated by Simon Patericke, [1577?], 1602.

I weigh not men, and therefore not men's words.
Admired I am of those that hate me most.
Though some speak openly against my books,
Yet they will read me, and thereby attain
To Peter's chair: and when they cast me off,
Are poisoned by my climbing followers.
I count religion but a childish toy,
And hold there is no sin but ignorance.
'Birds of the air will tell of murders past!'
I am ashamed to hear such fooleries.

*   *   *   *   *   *

Might first made kings and laws were then most sure
When like the Draco's, they were writ in blood.†

The scheming favorite who overthrows duchies with
his machinations and deceit—stock figure of the
tragedies and tragicomedies of three generations—
is the attempted realization of this bugaboo Macchiavelli by the imagination of Tudor dramatists.
Whole plays were penned on the subject: there was
a *Macchiavelli* on the stage in the nineties, a Latin
Macchiavellus about the same time at Cambridge.
The later *Macchiavelli and the Devil,* though lost,
still further accentuates in its title this popular
misconception. And it was to this that the wretched,
dying poet, Robert Greene, appealed in his famous
words addressed to Marlowe: "Is it pestilent
Macchiavellian policy that thou hast studied? O

---

†*Marlowe*, ed. A. H. Bullen, 1884-85, ii, 9.

punish folly? What are his rules but mere confused mockeries able to extirpate in small time the generation of mankind?"†

The Courtier is a very different book. Therein is presented an engaging picture of the little court of Urbino in the early years of the sixteenth century. There the graces of conduct and the virtues of kindliness abounded and a sweet and unaffected converse combined with innocent merriment, presided over by the grave but courteous duchess of that state. This circle was doubtless not so brilliant as the notable assembly which met in Florence at the fiat of Lorenzo the Magnificent, where Pulci, Ficino, Pico and Poliziano discoursed learnedly and eloquently of state, art, literature and philosophy. But at Urbino there was a comity of spirit, a "sweet conversation that is occasioned of an admirable loving company," to quote the translator, Sir Thomas Hoby's words; and while we may recognize in its externals traces of that worldliness, lightness and vanity which rise to the surface, like froth, on the current of any social life, it held before it wholesome and gracious ideals, honoring gentleness and delicacy in man no less than in woman and offering conclusive refutation to the charge that the Italy of the renaissance was hopelessly abandoned and corrupt. Further into these larger literary and political influences in

---

†*A Groatsworth of Wit*, 1596; Saintsbury, "Elizabethan Pamphlets," p. 155.

Tudor times emanating from Italy, we can not enter. Let it suffice that we recognize how diverse and complex they were, how variously they were represented and misrepresented, and how they made for good quite as much, if not more, than they could ever have made for evil.

To one who has not had occasion to give his attention to the topic, it may seem surprising to learn how early Italian influences set in to determine the nature of English drama and how specifically these influences were directed into the time-worn channels that we know so well. For example, although most of the extant plays that survive from the fifteen sixties are either classical in subject from their origin at court, or vernacular from the rudeness of their unlettered authors who wrote for the scaffolds of the inn-yards, still the mania for Italian fiction arose in this decade and we hear of such things as this. In 1562 a gentleman named Arthur Brooke published a narrative poem which he had translated from the Italian of Bandello. He entitled his work *The Tragical History of Romeus and Juliet,* and in his preface to the reader he writes: "I saw the same argument (that is the same story) lately set forth on stage with more commendation than I can look for." As there is nothing to prove that this play, which Brooke so mentions, was a foreign play, we may conclude (with Ward, who long ago suggested it), that "the first English tragedy on a subject taken directly or indirectly from an Italian novel is based on the story of Romeo and Juliet"; and this was two years before the birth of Shakespeare. Once more, in the Stationers' Register, the official list of books permitted to be printed, between July, 1565, and a year later, there is record of the licensing of an *Interlude of the Cruel Detter* by Wager. It was formerly surmised that this may have been an earlier version of a play called *The Jew,* described in 1579 by Stephen Gosson, a pamphleteer of the day, as expressing "the greediness of worldly choosers (that is Portia's unsuccessful suitors in their choice of the caskets), and the bloody minds of usurers (Shylock's implacable pursuit of Antonio in *The Merchant of Venice* for the pound of flesh.) And though we must now give up the play of 1565, that of 1579 is sufficiently identified to make clear its connection as the probable source of Shakespeare's *Merchant of Venice* of at least fifteen years later.† If anyone is troubled by this scandalous disclosure of the unoriginality of Shakespeare, let it be remarked to him, and to him only, that that great genius never invented a story if he could help it; and that when he did, as in the case of *Love's Labour's Lost,* his success was indifferent. There is a prevalent notion that identifies originality as it is called with inventiveness,

† See *Malone Society's Publications,* "Collections, Parts IV and V, 1911, pp. 313 ff.

constructive ingenuity and the art of surprise. Few of our prevalent notions are more misleading. It has been thought, for example, that if you can clutch and retain an idea which nobody else has cared to clutch or retain; if you can work it up into a series of surprises that nobody could have foretold or as ingeniously distorted, getting that precious thing, the climax, in the right place and remembering a number of hard and fast rules about nemesis, dramatic irony, and foreshadowing, cross-actions, by-play, stage business and the like, that the result will be a drama. As a matter of fact, the result will be a mechanism with as much relation to life as a mannikin is related to a man. Shakespeare did not work in that way. The story, even the plot, were in themselves nothing important to him. His eye was on the vital men and women, his personages, without which there can be neither play nor story. Any sketch of action would do and his personages, once subjected to such an environment, came to live in their interrelations as men and women come to live in life. We can not write dramas in this day and generation of ours by following anyone, least of all Shakespeare. We are not only hopelessly and forever behind him; but his road is not our road; and ours, did we but know it, is straight before. But we must back to our road, for this matter of the revival of the drama is beside it.

The extant drama of the sixties shows several

varieties of plays directly influenced by the fiction
and the drama of the Italians.† Thus Gascoigne's
tragedy *Jocasta,* 1566, came from Seneca, if not
from Euripides, by way of the *Giocasta* of Luigi
Dolci, as the same English playwright's comedy,
Supposes, derives through Ariosto's successful
adaptation of Plautus and Terence, *I Suppositi.*
Bugbears of John Jeffere, of much the same date,
is an adaptation of Grazzini's *La Spiritata* with,
says Boas, "episodes from *Gl'Ingannati* and the
Andria of Terence."‡ And with these in English
came Latin plays at the universities such as the
annonymous *Hymenaeus* and Abraham Fraunce's
Victoria at Cambridge, both of unquestionable
Italian origin. A more original Latin drama,
though of the type, is the famous *Pedantius* of
about 1590. But to return, in 1568 several gentle-
ment of the Inner Temple, with one Robert Wilmot
their leader, contrived an ingenious Senecan tragedy
entitled *Tancred and Gismund,* basing their story
on one of the hundred Italian tales translated by
Thomas Painter in a book which he called *The
Palace of Pleasure;* whilst some ten years later,
George Whetstone, a small poet and adapter
of Italian stories, worked up his *Promos and
Cassandra* from one of the novels of Cinthio's *Gli*

---

†On these comedies, see R. W. Bond, *Early Plays from the
Italian,* 1911, Introduction.

‡Boas, p. 133 ff.

Hecatommithi "into two comical discourses" (as
he called his plays albeit little comical they are),
"for that," he continues, "decorum used, it would
not be carried into one." It is of interest to remember that this crude, tiresome, gross and awkward
old drama has the merit of having worked itself
free of Senecan and Plautine limitations. But the
prime distinction of *Promos and Cassandra* lies in the
fact that it was the block out of which Shakespeare
carved years later the significant figures of *Measure
for Measure.*

In the group of dramatists dubbed par excel-
lence by the critics "the predecessors of Shakespeare," Lyly's plays are classical and Italian in
more subtle ways than in the borrowings of plots
and the adaptations of personages. His draughts
on the classics are by way of theme: *Endimion,* the
story of the young shepherd of Mount Ida who
sighed for Cynthia, the moon; *Campaspe,* the tale
of the love which that fair captive inspired in the
heart of Alexander the Great and his famous painter
Apelles; *Sapho and Phao,* the infatuation of the
Greek poetess for an humble ferryman. In like
manner Lyly had recourse to Italian literature for
his graceful and courtly manners in handling their
classical myths, for the pastoral idea with its delicate employment of allegory directed towards contemporary happenings in the intimate circle of the
court, and for a certain decorative quality in style

and treatment that conforms to ideals of renaissance Italian art. As to the other "predecessors," Peele is the most important rival of Lyly, preceding him in the adaptation of Italian ideals in his beautiful *Arraignment of Paris* and in poetry of form surpassing him; Kyd is Senecan and his foreign contact is French rather than Italian. Greene is English and eclectic in his practices, however he may have touched Italian subject-matter in his *Orlando Furioso,* which is of course a dramatised episode of Ariosto's famous epic poem, and in his *Scottish History of James IV* which is not "Scottish," but derived from a novel of Cinthio. As to Lodge, in his fiction and lyrical poetry we know that his affiliations were French; in drama, he is at best but a shadowy figure; while as to Marlowe, save for the theme of *The Jew of Malta,* his genius is less touched with the subject and example of Italy than almost any poet of rank in the whole age.

And yet with this comparatively slight showing of direct Italian influences in the plays that were on the stage in Shakespeare's youth, it is not too much to say that the age was literally soaked in Italian literature and fiction. There is a famous passage of old Ascham, the tutor in King Henry's time of the royal children, in which he directs his shafts against the immorality of the lighter fiction, the *Morte Darthur* as well as these books made in Italy. "That which is most to be lamented," he says, "and there-

49

fore the more needful to be looked to, there is moe
of these ungracious books set out in print within
these few months than have been seen in England
many years before. And because our Englishmen
made Italians can not hurt but certain persons and
in certain places, therefore these Italian books are
made English to bring mischief enough openly and
bodily to all states great and mean, young and old
everywhere."†

The Palace of Pleasure, already mentioned, is
the typical Elizabethan example of a collection of
Italian *novelle,* as these brief stories of all sorts and
kinds were called. This book is described on the
title as "beautified, adorned and well furnished with
pleasant histories and excellent novels selected out of
divers good and commendable authors." It appeared
first in 1566 when Shakespeare and Marlowe were
scarcely out of their cradles, and was the work of
Thomas Painter, a schoolmaster of Sevenoaks who
had first projected his book as early as 1562. A
later complete edition contains one hundred and
one tales, partly translations from Boccaccio, Bandello and other Italian *novellieri* and their French
imitators, partly imitations of their work. This in
general is the character of the other like collections.
By the time that Shakespeare began to write there
were at least a dozen such, to say nothing here of

---

† *The Scholemaster,* ed. Arber, 1870, p. 81.

single stories and imitations of the like, derived
from other than Italian sources, all of them, in the
quaint phrase of the day "forged only for delight."
Among the more important there was Sir Geoffrey
Fenton with his *Certain Tragical Discourses*,
Thomas Fortescue with his *Forest or Collection of
Histories*, Whetstone's *Rock of Regard* and *Hepta-
meron of Civil Discourses*. There was Wotton's
Courtly Controversy of Cupid's Cautels, made up
of five tragical stories, and George Pettie who emu-
lated the title of Painter in calling his book *A Petty
Palace of Pettie his Pleasures;* while Bartholomew
Riche, if we are to trust his title, took his *Farewell
to the Military Profession* in eight novels. The
Italian authors the works of whom appear in these
translations are many. Thus Whetstone derives
mainly from the *Hecatommithi* of Cinthio; Riche
draws chiefly from Bandello, though both he and
Fenton appear to have derived not a little of their
material only mediately from Italy through the similar French versions of similar stories by Belleforest and Boisteau. Fiorentino and Straparola
furnished other material.

These tales were the obvious quarry of the English dramatists whither they resorted as naturally
as the sculptors of the renaissance resorted to the
marbles of Ferrara. The stories, too, be it remembered, were not always confined to contemporary
Italian life as in the case of Bandello; but ancient

history was drawn on as well as modern and "outlandish," and all was in the process Italianized. Thus for example, there are upwards of thirty plays extant and lost that disclose subject-matter paralleled in Painter's *Palace of Pleasure*. These range from Lucrece, Coriolanus, Timon and other classical subjects to the Italian tales of the *Duchess of Malfi*, and *Romeo and Juliet*, the French *Giletta of Narbonne* (original of *All's Well That Ends Well*), to Turkish Mahomet and Irene (three times employed by the old playwrights), and the English Countess of Salisbury. These thirty subjects were paralleled (if not actually the sources) in plays, the work of Shakespeare, Heywood, Webster, Fletcher, Marston, Massinger, Shirley and several lesser men, furnishing the entire material for a play or only, in other cases, an underplot or episode. If we look at this field of Italian influence on our drama at large it may be confidently affirmed that at least one third of our old plays from Tudor times to the Restoration "may be traced to Italian influences in one way or another."†

Even when plays are not modelled on Italian plots there is often a tendency to give an Italian atmosphere and color to the action by the names of the characters, allusions of place and other like means. The stock example of this fashion is Jon-

---

†On this topic, see J. Jacobs, in his ed. of *The Palace*, 1890.

son's *Every Man in His Humor* which appeared in the quarto of 1601, the scene Florence, and provided with an all but complete Italian dramatis personae. In revision for his folio of 1616, Jonson translated his comedy to England; and it is astonishing how few changes he needed to make to effect a complete English atmosphere. Lorenzo di Pazzi became Old Know'ell; Prospero, Wellbred; Thorello, Kitely; Biancha, Mistress Bridget; "a gentleman's house yonder by Saint Anthony's" is translated "at Justice Clement's house in Coleman Street." Hoxton, the Windmill in Old Jewry, Moorsfield, are named, and the work is done. Much nonsense has been written about Shakespeare's power of local coloring. This power he undoubtedly possesses in a high degree, but it comes from the suggestions of his sources and only the unimaginative commentator can think it needful to send him to Italy for the coloring of *The Merchant of Venice* and *Othello,* or to Denmark for his *Hamlet*. Shakespeare's personages are seldom foreigners. The insularity of Shakespeare's treatment of foreigners can be found in the Welsh parson and the French Doctor of *The Merry Wives* or in Fluellen, Macmorris and Jamy with their Welsh, Scottish and Irish brogues in *Henry V*. The heart and soul of Shakespeare's fidelity to life is after all his faithful rendering of Elizabethan manners and conditions and his interpretation of them in their larger essentials into a universal art.

In tracing a play through its foregoing versions as they appear in these collections, English, French and Italian, it is not always an easy matter to discover which was the probable original. In the case of Shakespeare, fortunately, such is his customary fidelity to his sources, that he is more readily followed among the minute variations that distinguish different versions, than almost any other dramatist. Thus, the tragical tale of the ill-starred lovers, Romeo and Juliet, had been told first in western Europe by Masuccio di Salerno, soon after 1470; by Luigi da Porto, in his story, *La Giulietta,* in 1535; and by Bandello, in his *Novelle,* in 1554. From the last, it was translated into French by Boisteau to form one of the stories of François de Belleforest's *Histoires Tragiques,* 1559. Three years later Arthur Brooke, as we have seen, translated the story into English verse; and, in 1567, it appeared in the straggling prose of Painter's *Palace of Pleasure.* If you like you may trace the essentials of the story back to a Greek romance of the second century entitled *Abrocomas and Anthia* by Xenophon of Ephesus, or forward to a Dutch version of 1630 by Jacob Struijs. But all this learning and the pursuit of the "saga" (as the Germans call it) with Teutonic determination to the days of the Pharaohs, Babylonia, or furthest Ind is to little purpose. When all has been said, Shakespeare's source was, as usual with him, the nearest;

54

and probably Brooke's English poem, not without a knowledge of the tale as related by Painter and Bandello. It is even more likely, as already suggested, that Shakespeare dramatized an old play of Brooke's mention which goes back to the days of *Gorboduc.*

Let us take another case, that of *Twelfth Night.* Here three stories, Italian, French and English, and four plays, three of them Italian, one Latin, are involved, to say nothing of incidents, Plautine and Terentian. Historically considered, this comedy was first referred back to a novel of Bandello which it remotely resembles; then to the version of the same by Belleforest; and still later to one of the stories of Riche's *Farewell to the Military Profession,* entitled *Apolonius and Silla.* It was then that a clew was discovered in Manningham's *Diary,* wherein that contemporary of Shakespeare compared the play which he went to see "to that in Italian called *Inganni*" or the Deceits. This set the scholars on search, and three comedies of this title were turned up by their industry. One was later than Shakespeare and so could be disregarded; the other two were that of Nicolo Secchi, at Florence in 1562, the other that of Curzio Gonzago, printed at Venice in 1592; but neither was sufficiently close in plot to make affirmation on the subject reasonably certain. However, the search went further, and Hunter discovered a still earlier Italian play *Gl' Ingannati* or the Deceived which had previously escaped notice because it was printed as part of a ceremony of sacrifice by a society called *Gl'Intronati* or the Thunderstruck, on the occasion of its first performance in 1531, and the general running title, *Il Sacrificio*, obscured the title of the play. This society of the Thunderstruck was apparently the author, or contained the authors, as well as the actors of *Gl' Igannati* and their play enjoyed considerable popularity in Italy, coming into print no less than four times before its story was retold by Bandello in 1554, finally reaching England in a Latin translation, entitled *Laelia,* acted in Queen's College, Cambridge, 1590, and again in 1598. Shakespeare's *Twelfth Night* has been dated by nobody earlier than 1599 and most authorities vary only a year or two after that date. It looks as if we had here found a direct source, Italian, or at least Latin, for a comedy of Shakespeare; and, as we learned in the last chapter, even the Latin may not have been a bar. But after all, if we sweep away the cobwebs of all this learning about the "deceits" of Italy, the Deceived and the Thunderstruck, a simple comparison of the plots of all the claimants involved discloses that once more Shakespeare did the obvious thing and went to the English version of Riche, *Apolonius and Silla,* for the dead material which he transmuted by the enchantments of his art into the charming comedy, *Twelfth Night.*

There is a beautiful passage on this topic by the late Dr. Furness, one of the best of Shakespeare scholars as he was one of the gentlest of men. It runs:

"But what false impressions are conveyed in the phrases which we have just used to express a process whereby Shakespeare converted the stocks and stones of the old dramas and chronicles into living, breathing men and women! We say he 'drew his original' from this source, or 'he found his materials' in that source. But how much did he 'draw' or what did he 'find'? * * * When, after reading one of his tragedies, we turn to what we are pleased to call 'the original of his plot,' I am reminded of those glittering gems, of which Heine speaks, that we see at night in lovely gardens, and think must have been left there by kings' children at play, but when we look for these jewels by day we see only wretched little worms which crawl painfully away, and which the foot forbears to crush only out of a strange pity."†

But definitely, now, in this age which was so literally soaked in the poetry, fiction, drama and arts of Italy, how did Shakespeare stand with reference to these potent examples? If we compare him at large with his contemporaries in whom we find these influences most active—with Sidney and

---

†*The Variorum Shakespeare,* "King Lear," p. 383.

Daniel in the sonnet, with Watson and Barnes as to other Italian lyrical forms, with Spenser in epic poetry, or with Marston, Chapman or even Ford or Webster in the drama, it may be affirmed that Shakespeare was far less affected by a direct contact with Italian literature than any of these. The Shakespearean *Sonnets* are singularly free from Petrarchanism, the darling sin of their species, and the erotic warmth of Shakespeare's narrative poetry is readily distinguishable from the sensuality and pruiency of its ultimate Italian models. In Shakespeare's dramas, Italian influences (defining the term loosely) are limited at best to ten or a dozen plays; and in most of them an English intermediary, poem or drama, is discoverable to explain his choice of subject. How deviously Italian is the derivation of the plot of *Twelfth Night* and the story of *Romeo and Juliet,* we have already seen. *Measure for Measure* we have heard of too, as derived mediately from Cinthio's *Hecatommithi* through Whetstone's *Promos and Cassandra;* and *The Merchant of Venice* is, with similar indirection, to be traced to a novel of Fiorentino's *Il Pecorone,* wherein the stories of the bond and the ring are combined, though here the intermediary English play is lost save for Gosson's mention. *The Taming of the Shrew* is a world story traceable in many tongues and versions; there is an older play extant which Shakespeare merely heightened and corrected. But the underplot of Bianca and her suitors is ultimately derivable from a comedy of Ariosto *(I Suppositi)* translated by Gascoigne as we have also already seen. One would scarcely think of *The Merry Wives of Windsor,* the only Shakespeare comedy of avowed English atmosphere, as Italian; and yet the main plot harks back to Straparola, however an English version *(The Lovers of Pisa* in Tarleton's *News Out of Purgatory)* may be cited to explain the dramatist's immediate quarry. The story of Helena in *All's Well That Ends Well* is to be found in the ninth novel of the third day of the *Decameron* of Boccaccio; Painter translated it. *Much Ado About Nothing,* that is the story of Hero and her discredit at the altar on her marriage day, is derived from the twentieth novel of Bandello; the story of the outrageous wager of his wife's honor by Posthumus in *Cymbeline* is from the ninth story of the second day of the *Decameron; Othello* is from the seventh novel of the third decade of Cinthio's *Hecatommithi,* though the sketch is very slight and only the beautiful name, Desdemona, occurs in the Italian original. Now, of these last three, to wit, the Hero story of *Much Ado,* the plot of the wager against Imogen's honor and the tale of "a Moorish captain who took to wife a Venetian lady," of these alone, have the busy commentators and amenders been compelled to confess that they find no versions in English in Shakespeare's time to which he might have had recourse had he desired to escape the reading of these tales in their original Italian or in the French version in which the story of Othello at least by his time had appeared.

Once more then we are confronted with the question of Shakespeare's learning; or rather, in this matter of the reading of Italian, with the question of one of his accomplishments. Even with these three untranslated plots before us, it is not absolutely necessary for us to assume that Shakespeare knew Italian. It is inconceivable that he should not have known the language of Boccaccio, had he at any time in his career found such knowledge necessary or desirable. But because we find Shakespeare treating an episode contained in the original Italian but not in any known English translation, or a story not translated until after the date of his play, we have not thereby a proof that he read Italian. With so general a knowledge of the language in England, and so many Italians sojourning in London, Shakespeare could have coped with any material which he may have desired to use. It is, however, interesting to observe that, save for *All's Well,* in this matter of Italian originals, as elsewhere, Shakespeare's earlier plays exhibit the almost certain intervention of some English play. Later he went further afield, borrowing freely from stories of Italian extraction, whether translated into his own tongue, transferred only so far as France or as yet untranslated.

Among Shakespeare's contemporaries and successors the Italian sources which he tapped were continually resorted to and they remained ever fruitful. Dekker, Middleton, Beaumont and Fletcher resorted to these sources much as Shakespeare had done before them, accepting the conventional background of Italian personage and scene, though they all drew like him from many other sources besides. Jonson little employed Italian story, save for the use that he appears to have made of Giordano Bruno's comedy, *Il Candelaio,* in *The Alchemist,* and of Macchivelli's *Belphegor,* together with a minor plot from the *Decameron* in *The Devil is an Ass.* The intricate comedies of George Chapman are of very varied, often composite, sources. One of them, *May Day,* is the making over in English of the Italian comedy, *Alessandro,* by Piccolomini, a popular success in its day; and Koeppel has found stock features of the Italian stage in *The Blind Beggar of Alexandria* and suggestions from Boccaccio in *A Humorous Days Mirth.*† Among the later contemporaries of Shakespeare, Marston is alto-

---

†On this general topic, see T. M. Parrott, *Chapman, Comedies,* 1914, where the material is well collected and epitomised; p. 674 ff. Also Stiefel, in *Shakespeare Jahrbuch,* xxxv, 180; and Koeppel, *Quellen Studien zu den Dramen Chapmans,* 1895 pp. 21-33.

gether the most Italianate. He quotes Italian familiarly, his scenes, personages, manners, all conform to Italian rather than to English standards. And yet, save for his use of two or three stories from that familiar source, Painter's *Palace of Pleasure* (*The Dutch Courtezan* and *The Insatiate Countess*) the precise borrowings of Marston seem indeterminable. *Antonio and Mellida,* especially the second part, and *What You Will* reproduce the atmosphere of the Italian *novelle* however the former, as *The Malcontent* and *Parisitaster,* add a certain grimness of mode not known to the easy and circumstantial manner of Italian fiction. It is with Marston that Elizabethan drama begins to breathe the air of that wicked and intriguing Italy against which Ascham had warned the youth of his day. But we may defer this topic for the moment.

Historical Italy remained much the image reflected in the Italian fiction of the day. Thus a lost play on the abandoned mythical female Pope Joan, was doubtless calculated to arouse a preverted Protestant zeal; *Tasso's Melancholy* may have told the romantic story of that great poet's passion for Leonore d'Este; and *Guido,* the career of the soldier of fortune, Guido Guerra, leader of the Guelphs in the Florentine broils of the thirteenth century. More interesting are the plays that stage almost contemporary Italian intrigues and scandals. Thus Middleton's *Women Beware*

Women has to do with the story of Bianca Capello
and Francesco de Medici, terminated by his death
at the hands of the Cardinal, his brother, in 1587.
Contemporary accounts of this scandal in high life
were brought back by travellers such as Fynes
Moryson, for example, who tells the story in his
Itinerary, the delightful result of one of the earliest
university travelling fellowships on record.† Even
more interesting is the similar story of crime and
intrigue involving the liaison of the Duke of Bra-
chiano and Vittoria Accoramboni which Webster
worked up into his master-tragedy *The White Devil
or Vittoria Corambona.* One of the most recent
editors of Webster's two great tragedies, declares
that "it is by no means certain that Webster made
use of any documents written or printed, as the
material for the plot of *The White Devil."* His
treatment of the subject seems the mingled true and
false report of a great case, brought to England by
some returning traveller; for the picture of Vittoria
which Webster presents is biased and most prejudi-
cial to that "ill-starred heroine." The critic goes on
to give examples of inaccuracies in the details of the
story, in the names of the personages involved, and
in the places of action; and he sums up: "On the
whole, I conclude that Webster gained his material
from some one who had heard much about the

---

†ed. Hughes, 1903, p. 94.

affair, and who, in recounting it, fell into minor inaccuracies besides being on the wrong side of the argument."†

It is accepted critical opinion that, save alone for Shakespeare, our old English drama produced no such master of tragedy in its gloom, its terror and inevitable tread to dreadful overthrow as this same John Webster. Companion play to *The White Devil*, with its brilliant and glittering picture of the daring, beautiful and shameless Vittoria, stands the pathetic figure of the Duchess of Malfi, sweet in her womanliness, noble in her steadfastness and endurance of intolerable torture of mind. The sources and parallels of this famous story, had we the time to dicuss them, would take us through half the literatures of Europe. There was Bandello, who first told this tale of two princely brothers in their vengeance on their sister for a marriage beneath her in station; Belleforest and Goulart in French; Painter, Beard and Grimestone in English; and after the date of Webster's play, Lope de Vega dramatised the story for the Spanish stage. The source of Webster's other tragedy is a recent scandal as we have already seen. Still another example of a *cause célèbre* is Massinger's *Unnatural Combat* in which that poet throws the emphasis of his plot on the strife and unnatural slaying of his son by

---

†Professor M. W. Sampson in *Webster's White Devil and Duchess of Malfi*, "Belles Lettres Series," 1904, p. xxx.

Francesco Cenci to the partial obscuration of his unspeakable crime against his unhappy daughter, Beatrice, who became her own avenger.

In these our dusty dealings with the old quarries whence were brought the bare hewn stones out of which to fashion works of genius, it has not been our business to linger on their finished perfections. The group of plays to which these two of Webster and *The Unnatural Combat* belong represent, if we except a play or two of Ford's, the most degraded pictures of renaissance depravity in our literature. In them and in Marston's two plays on *Antonio and Mellida* and his *Insatiate Countess,* in Tourneur's *Revenger's Tragedy* and *Atheist's Tragedy,* in Middleton's *Women Beware Women* and *The Changeling,* will be found that strange combination of the graces and amenities of the cultivated society of the Italian renaissance with its godless intrigues, its abandoned profligacy, its ingenious cruelty and callous onlook of the intellect while the passions rush in wild career to the utter perdition of body and soul. And more, all is told in these plays with a poignant realization of the momentousness of crime and its deadly consequences.

A suggestive essay, *The Italy of Elizabethan Dramatists,* attempts an explanation of this.† Nothing could exaggerate the moral depravity of this

---

†Vernon Lee, *Euphorion,* p. 57, and especially 71 and 72.

Italy of the Cencis and the Borgias nor the effront-
ery and ingeniousness of their crimes. And yet
these terrible personages, unlike the beastly early
Roman emperors, seem outwardly to have been
little transformed by their wickedness and were
often gentle in their manners, lovers of learning
and cultivators of the amenities of life. Moreover,
search as we may through the literature of the period we find nothing to suggest the fierce and violent
spirit which produced these lured outbursts of the
Elizabethan tragic genius. This Italian literature
is singularly free from terror and horror; it is
equable, serene, "a spotless art, a literature often
impure, but always cheerful, natural, civilized."
There are no deeps nor heights in it. When we meet
a tale of depravity in Bandello or Cinthio, it is told
with the same cheerful frankness, the same gossipy
ease which is applied to anything involving a momentary interest; for virtue and vice are accepted
equally as phenomena of this strange and inex-
plicable world of ours. An age which could take
joy in the tinsel sentimentality of the pastoral and
find its deepest emotion in the torpid melancholy
of Tasso, could produce no true drama. Its very
serenity, dispassionateness, moral indifference and
cynical aloofness, all were against it. Brought face
to face with these aberrations from the normal
trend of human conduct, it was not with this indifference that the northern, gothic mind reacted. Hor-

rified and fascinated, it translated that horror and
fascination into moral terms and infused into its
Vittorias, Bosolas, Vindicis and the rest a super-
human struggle of the agonized soul with evil, absolutely unknown to the facile consciencelessness
of the actual personages depicted. These overwrought tragedies of Marston, Webster, Tourneur
and Middleton, once or twice, were only possible to
the grim Puritan inherent in the English nature
and their monstrosity consists largely in the circumstance that no personage whose nature was so
Italianate as to plunge him into such fantastic wickedness as theirs could have been possessed of a conscience so searching or have suffered a remorse so
overwhelming. It was Ford, alone, somewhat later,
who "conceived of the horrors of the Italian renaissance in the spirit in which they were committed."
The abomination of his art lies "in the superficial
innocence of its tone, in its making evil lose its ap-
pearance of evil." Leaving Ford aside, for the rest,
this is stern stuff and no food for weaklings; and yet
this contrast is ever discernible, if we compare these
dramas of genius with the petty material from
whence they sprung; the plays have been raised to
the regions of poetry and into the sphere of a higher
art where the particular case, vulgar, hard and in-
tractable, has become transmuted into the universal
idea. We are affected, as in all true tragedy, by
the terror and the pity of it all, and, with a stand-

ard of true ideals before us, remain unsmutched by the sordidness, the filth and the wretchedness of these terrible realizations of human malignity, depravity and crime.

As we progress through the reign of King James, although plays in Italian setting and of Italian derivation continue, furnishing some of the strongest themes, the drama as a whole becomes less Italianate under the influence especially of Fletcher and Massinger and their new species of play, tragicomedy. Here although Italian names for the dramatis personae in some cases persist, the scene is often delocalized into some charming no man's land of Epire, Candy or Iberia, and the personages fall into types of larger groups. For example, the foreign sources of Massinger scatter from Suetonius, Plutarch and Josephus to mediaeval martyrologies and French and Spanish fiction. His *Unnatural Combat* is conspicuous in its employment of an Italian story, that of the Cenci. Shirley, too, is similarly omnivorous as to source and ecclectic in practice. In *Love's Cruelty* alone does he appear to revert to the old Italian quarries, here Cinthio; and his two most Italianate tragedies, *The Traitor* and *The Cardinal,* are referable to his Elizabethan predecessors for inspiration, not to a direct recourse to Italian history or fiction. As to Ford, Koeppel declares his work to be almost entirely free from Italian literary influences; and in-

deed Ford displays a certain pride and boastfulness
as to his originality more than once in his writings.
Yet none the less such is the Italian spirit of most of
his plays that Swinburne says of the most notorious
of Ford's tragedies: "The story of Giovanni and
Annabella was probably based either on fact or
tradition; it may perhaps yet be unearthed in some
Italian collection of tales after manner of Cinthio
and Bandello."†

There remain two subjects in our drama commonly referred to Italian originals: the masque and
the pastoral. As to the masque, it has been ques-
tioned whether such immediate foreign influences
as were exerted on that interesting by-product of the
drama, were not really more French than Italian.‡
The pastoral indubitably harks back in its earlier
specimens to Sannazaro, Tasso and Guarini and
through them to the spark dropped by Boccaccio
in his *Ameto,* 1478. Sannazaro's romance, the
Arcadia, Tasso's pastoral drama, *Aminta,* 1573,
Guarini's attempt to rival the latter in his *Pastor
Fido:* these are the sources and inspiration of the
group of English exotic pastorals in dramatic form
from Sidney's *Lady of May* to the four great English pastoral plays, Daniel's *Queen's Arcadia,*
Fletcher's *Faithful Shepherdess,* Jonson's *Sad Shep-*

---

†*Essays and Studies,* 1876, p. 276.

‡On this topic see R. Brotanek, "Die englischen Masken-
spiele," *Wiener Beiträge* xv, 1902.

herd, and Randolph's *Amyntas,* which lie between 1605 and 1635. The pastoral, at best is only an Italian "cockney's idea of the country," with its prating of the golden age, its nymphs, fauns and impossible virtues, its petty loves and petty hates; and it had never more than a qualified success in England, however, gentlemen of the court of Charles, such as Sir Walter Montague and Abraham Cowley, influenced by the example of France, revived it, to practice and approved it. There is no healthier use of the pastoral than that of Shakespeare who employs it in *As You Like It* both for embellishment and delicate raillery. The banished Duke in the Forest of Arden leads the life of Robin Hood, not that of the *Aminta;* except that Celia buys a sheepfold to elude pursuit, she is no shepherdess nor wishes to become one. Silvius and Phoebe are pastoral; but Corin, to say nothing of Shakespeare's own figures, Audry and William, are genuine English rural folk. Nor is the exquisite wooing of Orlando and Rosalind, but for its savor of burlesque, in any wise pastoral, but rather a diverting parody of the sentimentality of Arcadian wooing and love-throes.

To look back over the ground we have just traversed, Italian influences in our old drama were pervasive and exerted in many different ways. It was as the land of mediaeval romance that Italy inspired Greene's somewhat crude dramatization of the *Orlando Furioso,* one of the larger group of heroical dramas that disregarded alike the bounds of nationality, geography and reason. It was this species in English drama that Beaumont ridiculed in his *Knight of the Burning Pestle,* that refreshing parody on the absurdities of the heroical play. Another phase of Italian contact—for it was little more—came earlier, that was subject-matter inspired by the Protestant conflict. Already in 1529 there is record of a drama now lost, on *King Robert of Sicily* whose throne, it will be remembered, was occupied, he being unworthy, by an angel king and he rebuked for his impiety. More certainly controversial is the play dealing with the career of the Italian Protestant Francesco Spiera which Nathaniel Woodes set forth in his *Conflict of Conscience,* in 1560. It was not until the days of Lyly that Italian culture and refinement, the better spirit of the renaissance, came to affect English dramatic writing. It was characteristic of Sidney, paragon of the conduct, the chivalry and the learning of earlier Elizabethan England, that he should have suggested the introduction of the Italian pastoral ideal into England, as it was characteristic of Lyly, the Euphuist, that he should have applied Italian dramatic ideas in a more adaptable way to the entertainments at court. It was the popular dramatists, however, Shakespeare foremost among them, who utilized to the full the possibilities of Italian fiction, however indirectly much of it must have come to them; and it was Marston, Webster, and their kind who worked this mine, less for its romantic stories than for its ingenious intrigues, its tales of strange wickedness and appalling abandonment to the lust of the flesh and the malice of the devil. There is little question that as the age went on it demanded a stronger sensational diet and it was here that it found what it craved, not only by robustly heaping together horror upon horror but by, what was far worse, a pandering, in the brilliant but, some of them, degenerate plays of Ford, to a pruriency of taste which the cleaner age of Shakespeare had not known.

The direct effect of Italian drama on English drama came after the vogue of the Italian *novelle;* and so far as may be made out, it was exerted far more powerfully on the academic plays that flourished at the universities than on the popular drama of the London playwrights. Leaving aside the cursory effects of several Italian acting companies which appear to have visited London as early as 1582, we have only a few early cases of Italian comedies directly translated, such as Grazzini's *La Spiritata,* in English *The Bugbears,* 1561, or Ariosto's *Suppositi* in Gascoigne's translation, already mentioned. In the eighties and nineties it became quite the fashion to translate Italian dramas into Latin for academic presentation. Most famous among the tragedies so derived was William Alabaster's *Roxana,* a play extravagantly praised by Dr. Johnson in ignorance of the fact that it is a literal translation into Latin of *La Dalida* by Luigi Groto. Giovanni Battista , della Porta, a contemporary Neapolitan physician and dramatist, seems to have enjoyed among the collegians an exceptional vogue as a quarry for the material of academic plays. This was doubtless due to the success with which he drew upon Terentian and Plautine characters and situations, complicated in ingenious and novel plots. Walter Hawkesworth translated Porta's *La Fantesca* and *La Cintia* into plays entitled *Leander* and *Labyrinthus,* acted at Cambridge in 1598 and 1599. The latter is described as "occasionally so decidedly *contra bonos mores,*" that, to use the words of an excellent old critic, "we may almost wish it had been more so." Far more important than either of these plays was the famous *Ignoramus,* the plot of which is taken from Porta's *Trappolaria,* and the well-written and diverting English comedy by Thomas Tomkins, *Albumazar,* 1615, which owes much to the same Italian author's *L'Astrologo.* These comedies commonly unite with intrigue and disguise the element of satire, which often so overlays the original plot as to give to the result a quality wholly new. Lastly, we may add to all this the strong Italian influence exerted by the popularity of the Italian pastoralists, Tasso and

Guarini, at college, remarking that it is likely that many identifications remain to be made in the field of the Latin and English drama at the universities in Elizabethan and Stuart days by scholars who are so fortunate as to be versed alike in English, classical and Italian dramatic literature.†

Thus much for the veriest sketch of the weighty influences of Italian literature and life on our old English drama. The field is one of remarkable richness and one in which something remains to be done despite the able work of Koeppel and others. And yet in all this traversing of once fruitful fields, now long since reaped and mown and gleaned to the veriest last straw, we are reminded of the words which Dr. Furness applies to our subject from a lecture on anatomy by the Edinburgh Dr. Bradley: "Anatomy may be likened to a harvest field. First come the reapers, who, entering upon untrodden ground, cut down great store of corn from all sides of them. These are the early anatomists of modern Europe. Then come the gleaners, who gather up ears enough from the bare ridges to make a few loaves of bread. Such were the anatomists of the last century. Last of all come the geese, who still

---

†Boas' excellent book on English University Plays unfortunately is limited to the Tudor period. To Koeppel we owe most in the way of a gathering together of our knowledge of Italian sources together with the pointing of many hitherto unrecognized.

continue to pick up a few grains scattered here and there among the stubble, and waddle home in the evening, poor things, cackling with joy because of their success. Gentlemen, *we* are the geese."†

---

†*The Variorum Shakespeare*, "Othello," p. viii.

III

FRENCH INFLUENCES AT COURT AND ELSEWHERE

FRANCE, to the popular Tudor imagination, was England's traditional and hereditary foe. The chief glory of England's military mediaeval kings had been their victories on French soil; and the days of Crecy, Poitiers and Agincourt were freshly remembered, however saddened by the recent loss, in the days of Queen Mary, of Calais, last hold of the English on the continent, a loss at last accepted in the very year of the birth of Shakespeare. When England and Scotland were at odds,—as when were they not?—it was always France that aided and abetted the northern raiders; when civil strife raised its hydra-head in France, embittered now by religious differences, it was English gold and English troops that fought against constituted French authority. At last when Mary, Queen of Scots and sometime Queen of France, put forth her audacious claim to the throne of English Elizabeth, it seemed as if the old enmity had come to an issue of such deadly and all reaching import that the world must pause breathless in terrified anticipation of an event on which hung Protestantism, political freedom and the fate of three empires.

But if France was a foe and there was joy that

England had so often defeated her, she was also, to use Sir Philip Sidney's words, "that sweet enemy, France," whose charm once to know was ever to acknowledge it. The French, it was universally admitted, were gentle people, acquainted above other nations with those delicate amenities that make social intercourse an art in itself and worthy the practice. Moreover, the French were deserving respect for their learning, their arts, for the honorable place they had ever maintained in peace as in war, however vanquished at times in the latter by their hardier English cousins. And besides all this, France was a near neighbor, as determined and satisfied in her nationality as was England herself, as disposed to stand on punctilios as to her national honor, and even more prone than England had been as yet to take a prominent part in the game of international politics. We are always curious about the doings of near neighbors and hence French history —wound up as so much of it was with that of England—was from early Tudor times a subject of English interest and inquiry. It was in the midst of the reign of King Henry that Lord Berners translated the chronicle of Froissart; and far later in 1607, the more nearly contemporary chronicles of De Serres, Matthieu, Cayet and others were gathered up and compendiously translated by Edward Grimestone in his *General Inventory of the History of France.* It was books such as these, together

77

with the popular chronicle histories of England, the work of Halle, Grafton, Stowe and Holinshed (so far as these concerned the affairs of France), that formed the sources of contemporary drama in these topics; and that drama, as we shall have occasion to learn, is by no means contemptible.

Classical influences on literature must be in any age remote. They belong to a deep and forgotten past, to be reconstructed as best by the antiquary and archaeologist, and their associations are always bookish. Italian influences, too, as they affected English literature were remote, at least geographically if not in point of time. The actual affairs of the petty Italian states never excited any deep or general interest in Tudor times. Actual events Italian readily blended with fiction and story so as to assume the dilation and enlargement of romance; and it was these especially that served the purposes of the drama. On the other hand it was the history rather than the fiction of France that interested Elizabethan playwrights, where the French tongue was not acting merely as an intermediary in versions recommended to English readers by their accessibility or their modern tone. France was open to much the same influences, literary and artistic, as those which affected England in renaissance times. France was nearer to Italy and of closer kindred to the Italian spirit; therefore we find an earlier and speedier assimilation of the revived classicism of

the age, and we find this classicism more permanent
than it could ever have become in less formal and
less responsive England. Many developments in
species of the drama, in mode of treatment, even
in subject-matter, run parallel in the two countries,
a circumstance less commonly referable to borrowing than to common classical or Italian examples
working simultaneously in both. But let us get
on to particulars.

A comparison of the development of the drama
from early times in France with its similar growth
in England, discloses a far earlier enfranchisement
from the dominance of religious and moral plays
in the former country. England knows, in a word,
no such body of purely secular plays, *farce, sottie,
débat* and satiric *revues*, as that well known in
France. The height of this light mediaeval secular
drama, in which spoke the *esprit gaulois* as it spoke
in the contemporary familiar or comic anecdote,
is exampled in *Maître Pathelin,* in print by 1485.
It was not until past the middle of the next century
that a play of like indigenous English spirit was to
come; and *Gammer Gurton's Needle,* with all its
merits, falls well below *Maître Pathelin.* It was
between these dates, 1485 and 1553, that the first
direct influence of French drama on that of England
made itself manifest, and this influence was of two
different kinds. The arch entertainer of the court
of Henry VIII was John Heywood whose talents,

literary and musical, with an ability apparently to organize them in combination with those of others, alone raised him above the station of a court jester. All will remember Heywood's several interludes, most famous among them that of *The Four P's* which details a contest in imaginative lying between three worthies, a pardoner, a palmer and a 'pothecary, with the decision in the case rendered by a pedlar. This little piece is full of verve and satiric wit. Another of Heywood's interludes describes an altercation between a friar and a pardoner in the precincts of a church, which leads to a lively scrimmage in which the combatants are parted with difficulty by the curate and "Neighbor Pratt." A third tells how Tyb, the wife of Johan, contrives to send that unhappy man on "a derisive errand," and keep him busily engaged while she eats up a savory meat-pie in loving company with knavish Sir Johan the priest. These subjects are plainly labelled "made in France"; they are of the very essence of the *farces,* and each has been referred, as has other work of Heywood's, to its French source and original.† Heywood was often inventive and he sometimes bettered his materials; but when we consider the force of his example in what came after, the French popular farce must be reckoned as one of the early sources of English comedy. There is one

---

†See A. W. Pollard in Gayley's *Representative English Comedies,* 1903; and K. Young in *Modern Philology,* i, 1904.

other certain translation of a French *débat* besides
those of Heywood in earlier Elizabethan drama and
that is Robert Greene's version of the *Débat de Folie
et d'Amour* by Louise Labé known in literary history
as la belle Cordière.‡ This involves classical personages and courts comparison with Heywood's
Play of the Weather in this respect. The other
influx of French influence between *Maître Pathelin*
and *Gammer Gurton's Needle* is of humanist origin
and is referable to the French scholar J. Ravisius
Textor. The diverting little interlude called
Thersites, the story of a youthful braggart, who
flies at the sight of a snail to refuge behind his
mother's apron strings, is a translation from Textor.
Thomas Ingeland's *Disobedient Child,* a play of
what has been called the cycle of the prodigal son—
because ultimately referable to the parable—has
been claimed likewise to be no more than the translation of one of Textor's Latin comedies.

In our consideration of classical influences we
have already recorded how the first English comedy
Ralph Roister Doister, was referable to a free imitation of the *Menaechmi* of Plautus, the first English
tragedy, *Gorboduc,* to an application of the manner
of Seneca to a myth essentially English. Here although the literary examples were classical, the immediate stimulus has been claimed by Sir Sidney

---

‡S. Lee, *The French Renaissance in England,* 1910, p. 374.

Lee for France. In view, however, of the fact that, as long ago as 1515, Trissino had written his tragedy *Sofonisba* in true Senecan manner but in Italian blank-verse, it seems scarcely reasonable to refer *Gorboduc* of 1561 (which is also in blank verse and not on a classical subject), to the *Cléopâtre* of Jodelle which, acted some ten years before, combines rhyming decasyllables in three acts with rhyming Alexandrines in the other two. If further proof were needed that the first outburst of the Senecan craze in England was due to Italian rather than to French stimulus, we need only consider the parallel case of Gascoigne's *Jocasta,* performed, as written, under conditions precisely those of *Gorboduc* and an acknowledged translation of Dolce's *Giocasta.* Neither Jodelle, in point of fact, nor yet Grévin, his immediate successor, seems much to have affected any play in English. The former's subjects, Cleopatra and Dido, were obvious enough, and had been long popular in Italy. That Shakespeare should have written on Cleopatra and Marlowe on Dido is nothing to the purpose; that Jodelle's employment of Plutarch as a source should in any wise have led Shakespeare to the same fountainhead seems purely fanciful. To each, Plutarch's *Parallel Lives,* whether translated by North or by Amyot,† was the inevitable model.

---

†See Lee's claim, *ibid*, 386 ff.

It was the work of Robert Garnier, the successor of Jodelle and Grévin, that introduced a new wave of Senecanism into England. This influence is very definite; and it differs from the earlier, direct Senecanism chiefly in its greater refinement of taste, its improved literary quality and in a tendency to follow the French preference for rhyming verse. French Seneca never spread far; but it produced several dramas of considerable literary interest. It is familiar to all students that in England, as elsewhere in sixteenth century Europe, literature was fostered by noble and titled people in select little circles, devoted to the cultivation of poetry and much talk about it. Such a circle was the Areopagus club with its experiments in classical metres, presided over by Sidney who, it will be remembered, was the Countess of Pembroke's brother. Indeed it was in the wider reaches of this same circle that Gallicized Seneca came to flourish. Sidney himself died in 1586, too early to have taken any share in this; but his theories as to tragedy were well known as set forth in the *Apology for Poetry,* in manuscript some four or five years earlier, and they include not only severe strictures on the popular drama for its disregard of Aristotlean rules as to the unities, decorum and other matters, but a lament that even *Gorboduc,* which is otherwise praised, "is very defectious [and it] grieveth me because it might not remain as an exact model of all tragedies."

With such an ideal before her, the Countess of Pembroke set about translating Garnier's *Antoine,* published in 1590, and interested Thomas Kyd, whose patron she then was, in further translation of the great French Senecan. Kyd translated the *Cornelia,* but his promised translation of *Porcie* never appeared, his disgrace and death following soon after in 1594, the year of the publication of *Cornelia.* Neither this nor the Countess's tragedy of *Antoine* are notable achievements; both are "done into blank verse," and their literality brings out only too faithfully the conventional stiffness of their French originals. Samuel Daniel, earliest follower of Sidney in the Italianate sonnet and a graceful poet of recognized standing at court, appears to have undertaken tragedy with the encouragement of no less a sponsor than Edmund Spenser who was classical in his sympathies, as his correspondence with Harvey goes to show, and especially well versed in contemporary French literature. Daniel's *Cleopatra* owes much to Garnier's *Marc-Antoine,* however it purports to be an original treatment and continuation of Lady Pembroke's translation of that play. Garnier had carried the old classic tale to the death of Antony, Daniel made Cleopatra's suicide the goal of his tragedy. A kindred play is Brandon's *Virtuous Octavia,*

1598, which takes up an earlier period in the career of Marcus Antonius, that between his departures to the Parthian war and the fiasco at Actium. All of these plays are well written, as is Daniel's later *Philotas* and a belated specimen of the same limited group, Lady Elizabeth Carew's tragedy of *Mariamne* (1613, a subject in French of Hardy); but neither the graceful mediocrity of Lady Pembroke, the more adequate dramatic fire of Kyd nor the poetic spirit of Daniel could redeem these precise and "precious" specimens of an artificial and exotic art from the charges of frigidity, lifelessness and essential failure.

But the story of French Seneca is not yet fully told, and the name of one man of genius finds place in its otherwise mediocre annals. At what precise time Fulke Greville, later Lord Brooke, and owner of Warwick Castle, wrote his tragedies must remain uncertain; though it could scarcely have been later than this last decade of Elizabeth's reign within which nearly all these specimens of Gallicized Seneca fall. Greville was the boyhood's friend and associate of Sidney and he had shared in the experiments of the Areopagus club. Moreover he had enjoyed with a steadiness almost unexampled the favor of Queen Elizabeth; and he left behind him a beautiful book of tribute to his friendship and association with these two master-spirits of his time which he called a *Life of Sidney*. Therein Greville tells

85

us how he had consigned a play of his on *Antony and Cleopatra* to the flames that it might not be "construed and strained," like Daniel's *Philotas,* into a commentary on the passing events of the Essex conspiracy. This subject, even if we had not his personal relations, sufficiently connects Greville with the school inspired by Garnier. Greville's extant plays are *Alaham,* about 1600, and *Mustapha,* possibly rewritten as late as 1606. Both draw on the annals of the Ottoman empire, the latter possibly through the Frenchman De Thou's *Historia sui Temporis,* though Knolles' *General History of the Turks,* 1603, seems a more likely source. The terrible annals of the Turk had been employed long before by Kyd and others as material for tragic treatment, and this very story of Mustapha had been staged in Paris as long ago as 1561 under title *La Soltaine.* But this is not the source of Greville's tragedy. In structure, style and general content, Greville is strictly enough a disciple of his school; but he combined with all this a theory wherein he disclosed it as his purpose "to trace out the high ways of ambitious governors and to show in the practice, that the more audacity, advantage and good success such sovereigns have, the more they hasten to their own desolation and ruin."† Greville

---

†On this topic see M. W. Croll, *The Works of Fulke Greville,* Pennsylvania Thesis, 1903.

contrived, with this difficult theory and his imprac-
ticable model, to produce tragedy of a remarkably
high order poetical, emotional and dramatic. In
this strange atmosphere several of Greville's personages live as it is not the wont of the personages
of Senecan tragedy to live. There is one other follower of French Seneca to name, and that is Sir William Alexander whose four *Monarchic Tragedies* as
he called them, on Darius, Croesus, Caesar and the
contentions that ended Macedonian supremacy in
Alexandria, were printed in the years immediately
following the death of Queen Elizabeth. There is
apparently no reason to suppose that either these or
Greville's plays were ever staged or intended to be
staged. With them ended, save for a few sporadic
examples at the universities, any attempt to bind
English tragedy by Senecan rules until the genteel
efforts of Joseph Addison in his *Cato* a century
later. It was Monsieur Voltaire who, setting sail
on one occasion northward from France, made the
happy discovery of the barbarian island of the
English and of the barbarian poet, Shakespeare,
who at sometime lived therein. And it was likewise
Monsieur Voltaire who declared that Addison's
Cato, for its careful preservation of the unities and
for its merits of style, must be declared "the first
reasonable tragedy in the English language."

Let us turn now again to the popular drama.
It is sometimes forgotten that Shakespeare is the

most patriotic of English poets. Of no other can it
be said, as truly of him, that he devoted practically
a third of his dramatic activity to the celebration
of the historic deeds of his fellow-countrymen. It
would be difficult to find in any other literature a
parallel to the august series of Shakespeare's chroni-
cal histories in which, in ten stately dramas, glorious
with the pomp of state and the pageantry of war, he
tells in epic dialogue and action the triumphs, the
woes and memorable deeds of English kings and
English nobles. With *King John* as an outrider
before, and *King Henry VIII* after, these plays fall
into two tetralogies, telling continuously the fortunes
of England's royal houses of Lancaster and York,
from the paltry Richard II, whose weakness lost
him his crown, to the capably wicked Richard III,
overthrown from the excessive abuse of his own
ravening power. In four of these plays not only is
a large part of the action in France, but French
sovereigns, nobles and other personages figure as
an important foil for heroic English action; and
the events of French history—told often, it is true,
as English chroniclers had distorted them—enter
into the very fabric of the play. There is perhaps
no more glaring example of this last than the distorted picture of "La Pucelle" otherwise Joan of
Arc, who figures in the first part of *Henry VI,*
vacillatingly as the inspired peasant she was, again,
as a witch in communion with fiends and as a

maid abandoned and unchaste. There is a fine passage in *Pierce Penniless his Supplication to the Devil,* bearing date 1592, in which the author, Thomas Nash, bursts forth: "How would it have joyed brave Talbot (the terror of the French) to think that after he had lain two hundred years in his tomb, he should triumph on the stage and have his bones new embalmed with the tears of ten thousand spectators * * * who, in the tragedian that represents his person, imagine they behold him fresh bleeding!"† It is these scenes of the deeds of Talbot that stand out in this very play of the first part of *Henry VI,* which we have good reason to believe was revised from an earlier chronicle history of Henry, now lost, by Shakespeare about this very date. What finer tribute could we have to the power of his hand even at this early period. And is it not possible that the heroism and humanity, discoverable in the inconsistent portrait of the heroic Maid of Orleans, may be Shakespeare's effort to alleviate the horrid outlines of a picture, distorted by the traditions of national hatred for one whom an English tribunal had condemmed to the stake as a witch?

In all three of the plays that deal with pious, incapable Henry VI, beside him moves the terrible, —at last, in *Richard III*—the pathetic, figure of

---

†*Shakespeare Allusion Books,* 1909, i, p. 5.

Henry's queen, Margaret of Anjou, "the she wolf of France." We meet her first in her young beauty, captivating the heart of her captor, the Earl of Suffolk; then as queen, imperiously ruling with her paramour her weak and royal husband and the council of his realm; then deprived of her lover and defiant of her foes, exulting with cruel mockery in the murder of her enemy, the Duke of York; at last, bereft of her only son, discrowned, wretched and abased, bewailing with two "fellow queen's of England" the ruin of her wicked, ambitious life. There are greater and more artistic pieces of historic portraiture in Shakespeare; there is none quite so detailed and in a sense so complete. Margaret may almost be called the thread of evil fate running through these four epic dramas of the Wars of the Roses; the nemesis of evil that crushed and defeated France sent back into the heart of her foes, there to embroil, embitter and undo in civil warfare three generations of English men.

Henry V is the crown of the Shakespearean chronicle plays, its theme the brilliant conquest of France by that hero king. Throughout, the French are drawn as boastful, pleasure-loving and contemptuous of their austerer, colder-blooded foes; although, as always in Shakespeare, there are no more gallant, courteous or more truly gentle folk than these nobles, whether French or English, of mediaeval times of chivalry. Nowhere did Shake-

speare so feel the limitations of his petty stage, with
its dim appurtenances of make-believe and tinsel.
"O for a muse of fire," he exclaims in well-known
lines of the prologue to *Henry V:*

> A muse of fire that would ascend
> The brightest heaven of invention,
> A kingdom for a stage, princes to act,
> And monarchs to behold the swelling scene!
> Then should the warlike Harry, like himself,
> Assume the port of Mars; and at his heels,
> Leash'd in like hounds, should famine, sword and fire
> Crouch for employment. But pardon, gentles all,
> The flat unraised spirit that hath dared
> On this unworthy scaffold to bring forth
> So great an object. Can this cockpit hold
> The vasty fields of France? or may we cram
> Within this wooden O the very casques
> That did affright the air of Agincourt?

Save for plays on kindred sources and those that
Shakespeare remodeled, few of the chronicle plays
of his fellow playwrights touch English warfare in
France. Heywood's *Edward IV* perfunctorily treats
that monarch's abortive expedition of 1468 into
France; Edward III's exploits are subordinated to
less war-like, and less conquering, love-adventures
at home in the play of that title. In France the
history play, analogue of the English chronicle play,
had long existed. There were acted plays on Joan
of Arc, on the supposed Trojan invasion of France,

on the deeds of King Chilperic and his queen Fredegonda; and, almost contemporary with the events, there were plays on the civil wars, *La Guisiade, Le Guysien,* and *Le Triomphe de la Ligue.* An extension of this representation of contemporary domestic history was Montchretien's tragedy *L'Escossaise* which staged, in 1601, a little before *Hamlet,* the English trial of Mary Queen of Scots with her execution at Fotheringay. Whether inspired by the plays on the Guise, just mentioned, or independently of a knowledge of them, the initiative that strove to treat of French affairs in English drama chronicle-wise came apparently from Marlowe. His *Massacre at Paris* "with the death of Duke of Guise," was acted in January, 1593, and is probably the latest of his works. The text is corrupt and shows signs of haste in composition as well as marks of the interference of the censor. None the less in the violent Protestant conception of the colossal wickedness of the Duke of Guise, the masterful influence of Catherine de Medici, withdrawn as it is into the background, and her weak and treacherous son, Henry III; above all in the breathless haste of the action which details the consequences of St. Bartholomew rather than the events of that terrible night itself, this unsatisfactory play is not altogether unworthy its great authorship. *Henslowe's Diary* contains record just about this time of no less than three plays on the civil wars in

France. This subject, which was almost contemporary, was one of lively interest to Protestant England where partisanship with their Huguenot brethreen and the Huguenot champion, Henry of Navarre, ran high in these years. Unhappily these dramas have perished and we can never know to what extent they may have been indebted to the several plays on the Guise and kindred contemporary French historical subjects that flourished almost contemporaneously in France.

The one great Elizabethan who devoted his tragic muse to the celebration of topics derived from the history of France is George Chapman, more widely known as the famous translator of Homer. Chapman is a strangely unequal figure in our old English drama, now rising to a poetic power and a laconic wisdom only short of that of the very greatest of his contemporaries, and again blurring his images, stuttering, confused and failing where lesser men succeeded. Chapman wrote some half dozen tragedies in the last years of Elizabeth and within a decade thereafter, all of them, save perhaps one, referable to comparatively recent French history; and some of his figures live among the most successful specimens of dramatic historical portraiture of his day. Bussy D'Ambois, arrogant, unscrupulous adventurer and fatal duellist, raised to greatness by the whim of a Prince only to be hurried with equal levity by his princely creator to his ordained overthrow; Cleremont D'Ambois his brother a Hamlet-like man of study and contemplation, weighted and overwhelmed in the ungrateful task of avenging his brother's death; Charles, Duke of Biron, whose overweening pride and traitorous contumacy brought about his downfall; Chabot, Admiral of France, the pathetic story of a righteous man who, beset by enemies and practised on to his undoing, dies brokenhearted at the ingratitude of the sovereign he has served—these are some of the admirable historical figures of Chapman. And the dramatist has reproduced with effect the brilliant, if scandalous, courts of Francis I and the Henries III and IV, with their mines and countermines of intrigue, their atmosphere of heartless cynicism and their godless scorn of death and fate.

To these five plays, usually accepted as Chapman's, we may now add with some confidence, *Charlemagne,* first printed under title of *The Distracted Emperor,* by Bullen in 1884, and recently reprinted, much more in accord with the difficult manuscript text, by Professor Schoell of Chicago.†
According to the most recent investigations these five tragedies of Chapman which deal with all but contemporary French history range, in point of the period of their writing and first performance, be-

---

†A. H. Bullen, *Old English Plays;* and F. L. Schoell, *Charlemagne*, Princeton, 1920. See also the same in *Revue Germanique*, 1913.

tween 1603 and 1611.‡ Professor Schoell places *Charlemagne* at 1598-99 at latest. It may have been a little earlier, and is possibly the "French Tragedy by Chapman," registered for publication in 1660, as Bullen surmised. The use of a motif in *Charlemagne* subsequently repeated in Chapman's romantic comedy, *M. D'Olive*, and the derivation of this motif from Pasquier's *Recherches de la France*, 1596, one of the authorities later used for Chapman's other work of this type, makes this the more likely. The suggestion of French history for the subject-matter of this species of French chronicle play may well have come from Marlowe when we recall how Chapman reproduces the Marlovian superman in these plays and remember his completion of Marlowe's *Hero and Leander*.

As to sources, several contemporary histories by DeThou, Pasquier, Matthieu, de Serres and Cayet seem laid under contribution; for the story of Charles Duke of Biron, some of them quite closely, in other cases merely for hints and suggestions. But it would appear that here, as so often, there was really an English intermediary, as Professor Boas has shown, in Grimestone's *Inventory of the History of France*, 1607, itself a translation in composite of several of these writers.† As to much of the material of *Bussy D'Ambois*, most famous

---

‡See T. M. Parrott, *Tragedies of Chapman*, 1910, *passim*.
†First communicated to the *Athenaeum*, Jan. 10, 1902.

of these plays, Professor Parrott is of opinion that the dramatist must have had some of his story from current report rather than from written records. For the catastrophe of Bussy's life was not apparently in print even in France before Chapman had represented it in his own manner on the stage. In the sequel, *The Revenge for Bussy D'Ambois,* the author is even more inventive, not only in the creation and character of his hero, Cleremont, the "Senecal" brother of Bussy, but in a denouement in which is slain his Montsurry who, in the person of his original, Monsoreau, survived his demise on the English stage for several years.‡

In dealing with affairs so recent, Chapman did not escape the censure of the censor. We learn through dispatches of the ambassador at the English court how he complained to the royal council of the performance of one of these very plays, because it brought on the stage the Queen of France using "very hard words" to Mademoiselle Verneuil, and finally boxing her ears; how the actors persisting in acting the scene after his protest, the ambassador had caused three of them to be arrested; but, he concludes "the principal person, the author, had escaped."† Chapman had trouble later in getting his plays into print, and he writes in high indigna-

---

‡Parrott, as above, pp. 542 and 572, in particular.

†Von Raumer, *Briefe aus Paris,* 1831, p. 276; and Parrott, p. 591.

tion as to "the bitter informer before the French ambassador," whose act, he says, was "performed with the gall of a wolf and not that of a man."‡ The extant copies of the two plays on the Duke of Biron fully attest the justice of the poet's description of them as "these poor dismembered poems." Another play, *The Noble Spanish Soldier,* the work of Dekker and Rowley, detailed the same scandalous contemporary story of the altercations between the queen of Henry IV and his mistress the Marquise de Verneuil, but a translation of the scene to an imaginary Spanish environment sufficiently concealed its identity, so that it escaped the fate of Chapman's play at the hands of the diligent censor.

French historical topics now once broached for the popular stage, several like plays, some of them of note, soon followed. There was Fletcher's *Thierry and Theodoret,* 1617, a powerful if disagreeable tragedy derived from early French chronicles, not without some flashes of allusiveness to the knowing of contemporary events; and the same author's *Bloody Brother,* 1624, like the far later *Fatal Contract* of Heming, seem similarly based on the atrocities of Merovingian annals. With a lost play on the Guise by Webster and another on the reign of Lewis XI, this enumeration of old English drama treating of historical France finds end. On

---

‡See these letters of Chapman published by B. Dobell, *Athenaeum,* 1901, p. 433.

the border land of pseudo-history, a frontier, be it remembered, that usurped far more of the empire of accredited fact than our captious and unbelieving age will allow, are several dramas purporting to deal with France: *The Weakest Goeth to the Wall,* 1600, an Italian story given a fictitious French historical setting, *The Trial of Chivalry,* 1597, placed in the interval of an undeterminable truce between France and Navarre. In the realm of mediaeval romances such as King Arthur and his like, besides *Charlemagne* already treated as Chapman's, there is mention of *The Four Sons of Aymon,* equally referable of course to the famous cycle of French romances on Charles the Great.

Turning from history and romance, it is surprising to find how little English comedy concerns itself with French scene. There is scarcely a comedy in Elizabeth's reign, save two or three, which can be confidently referred to a French source except where that source may have been employed as a means to convey earlier Italian or classical material. Two comedies of Chapman, *Monsieur D'Olive* and *The Gentleman Usher,* are French in scene, and a plot or so of Fletcher and some others; but most of these are later. As to Shakespeare's *Loves Labour's Lost,* returning to history, Hunter found, long ago, in Monstrelet's *Chronicles,* the "parallel" of "a king of Navarre to whom a king of France was indebted for a large sum of money." The former was named

Charles, not Shakespeare's Ferdinand. Hunter assigned the date of the plot to 1427 and found "likenesses" to Shakespeare's in certain names such as Longueval and Beauraine in French history at large.† Much later, Sir Sidney Lee identified the names of Biron and Longaville with those of "the two most strenuous supporters" of the famous sometime Huguenot king, Henry of Navarre, and that of Dumain with an anglicized form of Duc de Mayenne who was on the other side. Sir Sidney further finds in a conference, held at Saint Bris, in 1586, between Catherine de Medici and Henry, the inspiration of the play and suggests that Catherine's embassy in behalf of her decrepid son is not unlike the embassy of Shakespeare's Princess of France for her dying father; although he hesitates to affirm that Shakespeare attempted to depict the now aged Catherine in the form of his marriageable young Princess.‡ And now comes Professor Abel Lefranc to refer all these matters to the meeting, at Nérac, in Aquitaine, in 1579, between Henry and his wife, Marguerite of Valois, in which with much revelry, gallantry and intrigue, similar differences between France and Navarre were discussed and a treaty agreed on, not between the royal husband and wife, but with Marguerite's portentous mother, Catherine de Medici, who was present—very un-

† Hunter, *New Illustrations of Shakespeare*, 1845, i, 256.
‡ First broached in *The Gentleman's Magazine*, October, 1880.

like the play—and a party of the second part, as
the lawyers say, if not of the first—to all the pro-
ceedings. M. Lefranc discovers in "the flying
squadron" of fair ladies who somewhat notoriously
accompanied this royal progress, the suggestion for
the three demure gentlewomen attendant on Shakespeare's Princess. And he finds, too, in Shakespeare's assuredly amateurish scenes of any court
life in this comedy, so remarkable a reproduction
of the atmosphere of the two courts of France—
about the revels of which history tells a very different tale—that he feels constrained to look for the
author of all this "realism" in one who had lived
in France and therefore could recount such things
without any effort of the imagination.† It may not
be impertinent to add that a still more recent "iden-
tification" carries the *locus* of *Love's Labour's Lost*
back to Titchfield Park in Sussex, referring the allusions of the play to certain events of Queen Elizabeth's progress of 1591, to Southampton's recent
attempt to take part in the French wars and to his
efforts to postpone his marriage to a granddaughter
of Burleigh.‡ But this at least is not "a French
source." In *Love's Labour's Lost* we have perhaps

---

†*Sous le Masque de Shakespeare William Stanley VIe Comte
de Derby*, Paris, 1919, ii, 89-103.

‡See an unpublished paper by A. K. Gray, read at the meeting of the Modern Language Association of America, Decem-
ber, 1922.

Shakespeare's nearest approach to France. I can not but regard as fanciful the idea of Sir Sidney Lee that Shakespeare owes any feature of his sprightly dialogue to his French contemporary, Pierre Larivey.‡ Not only is there no trace of any influence of Larivey's comedies on Shakespeare, but Shakespeare's repartee, his punning and playing with words, his very puerilities—for there are a plenty of them in *Love's Labour's Lost*—are all easily to be accounted for in his direct imitation of all these things as he found them in the comedies of English John Lyly.

The question of Shakespeare's conversancy with French has been often raised. There is a whole scene in that language in *Henry V,* and many scraps and sentences elsewhere; the French is indifferent and might have been supplied him by an obliging acquaintance: such an acquaintance, in one Mountjoy, peruquier or wig-maker, we now know that Shakespeare had. He resided in Mountjoy's family for a number of years, at the corner of Silver and Monkwell Streets in the parish of St. Olave not far from Cripplegate and at a time when he must have actually been engaged in writing some of these historical plays.† Such another acquaintance may have been Italian John Florio, translator of

‡*The French Renaissance*, 423 ff.
†C. W. Wallace, *New Shakespeare Discoveries*, *Harper's Magazine*, March 1910.

Montaigne's *Essays,* a copy of which in the British Museum was long thought to contain a genuine signature of Shakespeare. It was from Montaigne and doubtless in this very translation that Shakespeare found the thought concerning an ideal state or commonwealth, put into the mouth of Gonzago, the wise old counsellor in *The Tempest.* Florio, like Shakespeare, found a patron in the Earl of Southampton. The scene of *All's Well that Ends Well* is in part laid in France. The Forest of Arden has been by unimaginative commentators construed into the Forest of Ardenne. Moreover Amiens, Jaques and other names of personages in Shakespeare are French, often mispronounced with the right that belongs to conquest, or at least misstressed by the imperial laws of his metre. We know that Ben Jonson once journeyed over to Paris, and, like some others since his time, behaved disgracefully there; we have no such knowledge as to Shakespeare. In a word, there is less that is actually French in his plays than Italian, and nothing that may not have been learned by the intervention of books or hearsay.

Scarcely anything seems more certain than the absolutely negative results of attempts to establish a single instance of direct contact between the popular French stage and that of England until we reach the immediate predecessors of Molière. Sir Sidney Lee, who had labored most ingeniously at the task of establishing parallels in this field, has noted that a French tragedy of popular type entitled *Philonaire*, acted in 1560, three years before Shakespeare's birth, tells a revolting story not unlike that of *Measure for Measure;* and that in a romantic comedy, *Lucelle,* by Louis le Jars, a poisoned draught, that turns out harmless, is administered much as in *Romeo and Juliet,* but to Romeo, not to Juliet, who appears to have been more prudent in France. Sir Sidney further finds that Larivey often employs "the sort of misconception as to the lady's identity which leads to Bertram's intimacy with Helen in Shakespeare's *All's Well,*" and that such episodes are employed for "unabashed merriment in Larivey's plays;" which, be it remarked, they never are in Shakespeare's.† Add to this that Larivey uses disguise much as Shakespeare in *Twelfth Night;* that Alexandre Hardy tells in comedies the story of *The Two Gentlemen of Verona* and of *The Winter's Tale,* both *after* Shakespeare, and of *Coriolanus* in 1607, a year before him, and we have the sum total of these endeavors. And let us pause before we leave this matter. Not one of these parallels establishes the slightest evidence relating to actual contact either one way or the other. Each of these Shakespeare plays is certainly referable to sources, none of them French; and every French play named above, with equal certainty, is refer-

---

†Lee, as above, pp. 408-411.

able to sources unEnglish, save only for Hardy's *Pandoste* which he had, like Shakespeare, from the prose romance, *Pandosto* of Robert Greene, translated into French before him. In these our *Quellen-Studien,* or, perhaps more appropriately here, in this our pretty game of *cherchez-la-source,* there are rules of conduct as in other games. While it may be true that a sufficient number of straws, judiciously and cumulatively piled, may break a camel's back, humps and all, it does not follow that any number of possibilities can by their accumulated weight make a probability, or that possibilities, however judiciously juggled, can permanently carry conviction where actual evidence is insufficient. All things are possible to God—and to the ingenious seeker after sources. And the thing would be merely ludicrous and so to be dismissed from serious consideration, were it not that much of our scholarship is tainted by this mania to descry and blazon to the world the essential unoriginality of man.

To recapitulate and in brief these French influences: thus far we have found a vital transfer of the spirit of mediaeval secular drama in the interludes of Heywood, back in the reign of Henry; and, in the nineties and for a few years thereafter, an unmistakeable influsion of Seneca into English drama as the French Robert Garnier understood Seneca and imitated him. Both of these influences were at court and only the earlier could in any wise sensibly have affected the drama to come. On the popular stage Shakespeare, the great experimenter, chose a French scene and French names for his personages in *Love's Labour's Lost,* his imitation of the allusive court drama of Lyly, and endowed with life the French, as well as the English figures, in his noble series of chronicle histories. In this same fertile period of the nineties, Marlowe pointed the way to a chronicle play dealing solely with French annals, and Chapman, his personal friend, continued his work in his able tragedies dealing with contemporary French politics and life at court. Neither Shakespeare nor Chapman was in this wise vigorously followed, and only a few, scattering influences of the cycles of old Charlemagne romances and possibly some French fiction is elsewhere discoverable. When all has been said, the effect of French poetry, prose and fiction on English Drama in the reigns of Elizabeth and James was decidedly small; outside of French history, so small as to be negligible; and the influences of French contemporary popular drama on the same kind of English drama during this time is actually nil.

With the accession of Charles I in the year 1625, nine years after Shakespeare's death, a change came over English drama. Shakespeare was still constantly acted and Jonson, though his best dramatic work was done, was at the height of his fame as the literary dictator and the accepted entertainer at

court with his sumptuous and splendid masques.
On the popular stage, Fletcher was all the vogue,
and in Fletcher's work, complete by 1625, we find
increasing traces of the influence of French literature, though not as yet of the French stage. It was
the presence and influence of the new queen of
Charles I, Henrietta Maria, that brought France
into the English mode. As a princess in her native
France and at a formative period of her life, Henrietta had been subject to the influences of the salon
which the Marquise de Rambouillet had founded
to protest against the rudeness of speech and manners which had come to characterize the court of
her time. The outcome of the "movement," as we
should now call it, was "the preciously written love
encyclopædia in the form of a novel," *L'Astrée*, by
Honoré D'Urfé, 1610, a work already employed by
Fletcher as a source for his tragedy *Valentinian*,
about 1618, and for an episode in his earlier comedy, *Monsieur Thomas*. Without here going into
particulars, Queen Henrietta brought four things
into English drama: the high-flown heroic romance
as a source for plays with its attendant cult of
Platonic love; the pastoral drama in a revived
French form; a Gallicizing of the masque, up to
that time largely an endigenous English growth; and
troupes of actors from her own country, who in time
wrought innovations in the conduct, scenery and
acting of English plays, most notable among them

the employment in time of women instead of boys in the roles of female characters. The masque as a by-form of the drama we shall have to neglect; the exalted ideas that led on to the heroic drama of Dryden were so weighted with Spanish influences that they will be best treated in our final chapter. Platonic love, in its genuinely lofty ideals as in its cynical perversions and ridiculous parodies, came straight from France; and, after a play or two by Davenant and others, about 1635, and some serious and humorous satire by Jonson, expired of its own inanity. As to the romances of D'Urfé's successors, the Scuderys, La Calprenéde and the rest, they soon became the common sources and inspiration of the decadent romantic tragicomedy, affected by court-iers such as Carlell, Lower, the Killigrews and even by Suckling as by lesser men, which grew up beside the still vigorous and still vernacular, if belated, Elizabethan drama of Massinger, Ford and Shirley. When all has been said, it must be admitted that the intimate interrelations of English drama with the vital drama of France practically began in the days of the Commonwealth when the great impetus that made Marlowe, Shakespeare and their celebrated suc-cessors had exhausted itself. It was in the sixteen fifties that Sir William Lower translated a couple of the tragedies of Corneille. Carlell followed him soon after, and by the date of the Restoration "sev-eral persons of honor," as they designated them-

selves, Waller, Sedley, Filmer and the Earl of
Dorset, were busy in the field of translation from
the French. And now came the active and incomparable genius of Molière who took by storm the
English dramatic world as he had carried nearly all
before him in his native country. No one foreign
author has been so plundered by English playwrights as Molière, and none has, as a rule, so suffered in the process. Molière's humane spirit, his
naturalness, adaptability and dramatic aptitude
were as much above his imitators as his verve, his
buoyancy, his ease and success of plot were beyond
the possibility of imitation. The attempts of
Davenant, Dryden, Sedley, Vanbrough, Crowne and
Shadwell to approach this incomparable original
fall beyond the range of our subject, as their talents
at their best fell short of the genius of this greatest
of the comedians. Let us leave this topic of the
influences of France on our old English drama with
the acknowledgement of this great debt which, in the
close dramatic relations which the two countries
have maintained since then, has gone on ever increasing.

SPANISH INFLUENCES ON FLETCHER, AND AFTER

FRANCE was England's hereditary foe; Spain, in Elizabeth's day, was England's contemporary enemy. The struggle with France was historic. Except for some inglorious skirmish such as the Battle of the Spurs, a credit to neither party, or the recovery of Calais by the French, of which Englishmen did not speak, there had been few actual meetings of the two countries in arms since the days of Agincourt and the disasters that followed. In the matter of religion, until King Henry of Navarre found Paris "worth a mass," Huguenot success seemed a probability and Protestantism the likely faith of the France to come. With Spain England's relations were very different. In the time of Philip II, Europe still trembled at the thought of his father's threatened universal dominion. With a diplomacy for guile, ruthlessness and success the most consummate in Europe, with troops believed to be incomparable in bravery and discipline, and with the Indies pouring in steady streams of the gold of a new world, it is no wonder that the phantom of Spain bulked large to early Elizabethan England. Add to this that King Philip was "his most Catholic majesty," that he was morally abetted in his ambitions and his diplomacy by the still mighty power of the papacy, that in Spain men of other faiths suffered torture and death at the hands of that most formidable instrument of religious bigotry, the Inquisition, and we can see why Spain was terrible and feared as France had never been feared in England. Then came the defeat of the Armada, and England was undeceived. Spain was not all-powerful; and English valor was not dead. The giant now became food for plunder. Who does not know of the valiant deeds of Englishmen at sea and on land against the crumbling power of Spain? Let one of the old poets tell us the familiar story.

Spain's anger never blew hot coals indeed
Till in Queen Elizabeth's reign then (may I call him so)
That glory of his country and Spain's terror,
That wonder of the land and the sea's minion,
Drake, of eternal memory, harried the Indies.

      *   *   *   *   *   *

Nombre de Dios, Cartagena, Hispaniola,
With Cuba and the rest of those fair sisters,
The mermaids of the seas, whose golden strings
Gave him sweetest music, when they by Drake
And his brave ginges were ravished; when these red
    apples
Were gathered and brought hither to be pared,
Then the Castilian lyon began to roar.

      *   *   *   *   *   *

       When on ships
Carrying such fire-drakes in them that the huge
Spanish galleasses, galleons, hulks and carracks,

Being great with gold, in labor with some fright,
Were all delivered of fine red-cheeked children
At Plymouth, Portsmouth and other English havens,
And only by man-midwives: had not Spain, reason
To cry out, Oh *diables Ingleses!*†

But we must go further back than this for the
earliest English play, definitely referable to a Spanish source. This is the interlude of *Calisto and
Melebea,* on the stage in King Henry VIII's
day and based on the dramatic novel, *Celestina* of
Fernando de Rojas, first published about 1499. The
intervention even of a translation into French or
Italian has not been proved, popular as the *Celestina*
afterwards became. The story of Calisto details
the amorous pursuit by that young gentleman of the
fair lady Melebea, aided by the go-between, a hag
named Celestina. In the original, the story proceeds
realistically and ends tragically. The English
adapter, with moralities his chief competitors on
the stage, shrunk from the catastrophe and ended his
play with a moral lecture. *Calisto* is remarkable,
considering its early date; the characters are clearly
distinguished, the dialogue lively, the construction
far beyond its English contemporaries; and it played
its part in helping to free the interludes and moralities of its time from abstraction and unreality.
Strange to say *Calisto and Melebea* led to nothing,

---

†Dick of Devonshire," I. 2, ed. A. H. Bullen in *A Collection
of Old English Plays*, II. 13-15.

although it anticipated the romantic drama that was evolved out of similar Italian fiction by at least thirty years. Perhaps this sporadic example of an English play in Tudor times, inspired directly by the literature of Spain, is best referred to the visit to England of the famous Spanish humanist, Juan Luis Vives, friend of Sir Thomas More, whom Henry placed as reader in rhetoric at Oxford, but whom he imprisoned and banished when he found him of the party of his fellow country-women, Queen Katherine, that unhappy lady who was divorced after twenty years of married life to make way for Anne Bullen, mother to be of Queen Elizabeth. Vives is known to have placed the Spanish *Celestina* amongst interdicted books in one of his writings; the moral ending in the English version may not impossibly have met with the Spanish humanist's approval. This matter, however, is pure surmise.

Passing onward to the range of actual Elizabethan drama, we find a scattered employment of Spanish scene and subject-matter, real or apocryphal. Kyd's *Spanish Tragedy*, like its imitation or burlesque the so-called *First Part of Jeronimo*, purports to be derived from Spanish annals. No real source has as yet been found for either play. *Lust's Dominion*, perhaps otherwise the earlier named *Spanish Moor's Tragedy*, has to do with two kings of the Peninsular and a malevolent moor, shamelessly plagiarized from the Aaron of *Titus Andronicus*. Peele's *Alphonsus of Aragon* is a composite of the biography of at least two sovereigns of that name. In his *Edward I* is contained one of the most cruel and unjust perversions of historical truth of which our old drama was guilty. This is the outrageous transformation of the charitable and estimable queen Eleanor of Castile into a monster of craft and wickedness. Somewhat less unhistorical is the same dramatist's *Battle of Alcazar* in which, as in part of an anonymous and later play called *Captain Stukeley*, is told the tragic fate of Dom Sebastian of Portugal. Among lost plays mentioned by Henslowe in his *Diary* there was another *King Sebastian*, a *Conquest of the West Indies*, an *Earl of Gloster* "with his conquest of Portugal," and a *Conquest of Spain by John of Gaunt*, the two latter clearly unhistorical "histories," calculated to please an English crowd whose appetite for stories of English valor abroad craved more examples than even the defeat of the Spanish Armada could afford them. As to that great theme, it recurs again and again in these plays, in allusion, told indeed in epic wise as in the passage quoted above, of which there is considerably more, and elsewhere rather lamely, as in Heywood's *If You Know Not Me You Know Nobody*. Perhaps the topic was too near the event; though, strange to say, in this very drama of Heywood's, Philip II is represented in person with dignity and respect. It was vivedly recalled that Philip had really been a sovereign of England. His name and effigy were still on current coins. It was as the husband of the English Queen Mary, Elizabeth's predecessor on the throne, that the enemy of England was here remembered. A lost *Philip II* of much the same period (the close of Elizabeth's reign) may have been of somewhat different content. But this we do not know.

Turning from these attempts to represent recent events touching Spain and Spanish personages on the stage, we find some dramas, strictly Elizabethan, the sources of which have been traced to Spanish influences. It is to be noted that they are exceedingly few and that the indirection rather than the directness of the channels of their transmission is the noticeable feature. Thus Marlowe's *Tamburlaine* is said to have been partially drawn from Pedro Mexia's *Silva de Varia Leccion;* but Mexia's book was already widely known in Italian, in French and in an English translation by Thomas Fortescue, (1573), long before Marlowe came to write. The story of Proteus and Julia in Shakespeare's *Two Gentlemen of Verona* is that of Felix and Felismena in the *Diana,* a pastoral romance of the Portuguese-Spaniard Jorge Montemayor. But the record of a lost play entitled the history of *Felix and Philiomena,* taken together with Shakespeare's

well-known predelection for taking for his dramatic
work the short-cut of an intervening play, should
dispose of this "Spanish source" forever.† Other
Shakespearean examples of "Spanish influences"
cited by the critics, are correspondences between
the *Comedia de los Engaños* of Lope de Rueda and
Twelfth Night, between a tale of *El Conde Lucanor*
and *The Taming of the Shrew,* and between the
fourth chapter of a collection of tales entitled
Noches de Invierno by one Antonio de Eslava and
The Tempest.‡ But, as we have seen as to two of
these cases, there is a nearer, easier, safer and more
reasonable derivation at hand; and as to *The
Tempest,* this ascription of a Spanish source, however confidently cited, is as yet by no means a settled
matter.

Spanish personages, of course, are scattered up
and down the Elizabethan drama, but for the most
part they are caricatures and "drawn with an un-
friendly pen." Illustrations are Middleton's Lazarillo (in *Blurt Master Constable*), a sad perversion
of that delightful rascal, Lazarillo de Tormes, Jonson's Don Diego in *The Alchemist,* an intention-
ally ridiculous, affected and bombastic falsification,

---

†See J. Fitzmaurice-Kelly, *The Relations between Spanish
and English Literature,* Liverpool, 1910, p 21, a pamphlet to
which I owe much.

‡See also J. de Perott, who finds an analogy, between *The
Tempest* and *El Caballero del Febo,* "Publications of Clark
University," October, 1905.

and Fletcher's lecherous paltroon, Prince Phara-
mond in *Philaster*. The boasters, Bobadil, Captain
Tucca, Ancient Pistol and the rest, there is surely
no need to seek them in Spain; for had the soil of
England produced none such, a clear literary
descent may be shown for them all from the *Miles
Gloriosus* of Plautus. Don Armado of *Love's
Labour's Lost* is Shakespeare's solitary burlesque of
the Spaniard; though it may be recalled that the
French, the Scots, the Welsh and the Irish, all are
represented in the defects and eccentricities of their
foreign speech by his kindly humor. It has been
suggested as to Don Armado, that he is a sketch,
from life, of an actual mad Spaniard, known to his
day as "fantastical monarcho." But if we will
look to Sir Thopas, an equally fantastic and grandi-
loquent personage of Lyly's *Endimion,* a drama on
the stage in Shakespeare's boyhood, we can find a
model for Don Armado, should Shakespeare have
needed such, with the Plautine line of boasters, already mentioned, so well known to him and to the
stage. The Prince of Aragon in *The Merchant of
Venice* is but a minor character. He chooses, it will
be recalled, with true Castilian pride, the silver
casket, because he will not "jump with common
spirits," and he takes his disappointment like a
gentleman. Portia's comment, so biting in other
cases, is solely on his deliberation. Shakespeare's
greatest Spanish personage is the English Queen

Katherine, so dignified and pathetic in her defence that she wins approval even of the heartless king, her husband, in his very repudiation of her. But in Katherine, racial traits yield precedence and fall away before that larger art that delineates with unerring stroke the universal lines of innocent wifehood, wronged and distressed.

All readers of the history of our old drama will remember that to Beaumont and Fletcher fell the popularity of Shakespeare on his retirement from the stage, a year, two or three as the case may have been, before his death. That Shakespeare formally or informally took Fletcher into collaboration seems as likely as the paucity of actual evidence can allow. That this association produced in the Shakespeare of *The Winter's Tale, Cymbeline* and *The Tempest* an artistic deterioration and a tendency to follow the example of his young apprentice, some at least still stoutly deny as contrary to the facts and to any inferences that scholarship ungifted with second sight can descry. Shakespeare had reached in these latter days the calm of harbor; that the waves no longer heaved with the heavy unrest of tragedy nor danced with the delight of frolicsome comedy, takes nothing from the blue of his later ocean or the quiet depths of those pellucid waters. As to Fletcher, it may be said first that he was an inventive genius, possessed of a far greater natural aptitude for stage-craft than any writer of his time, hardly even

excepting Shakespeare. It may be said, too, of
Fletcher that with the superlative success of the
greatest drama of modern times for his example, he
none the less succeeded in ringing new changes on
old themes and in giving by this means and by his
own invention a bias to the English popular stage
which lasted generations after him. Into the difficult literary relations of Beaumont and Fletcher it
is quite unnecessary to enter here. Let it suffice
to recall that Beaumont, who was twenty years
Shakespeare's junior, died in the year of Shakespeare's death, and as a matter of fact really before
him; secondly that Fletcher survived Beaumont
nearly ten years and collaborated latterly with
Massinger. Now, among the several new things
that Fletcher did in drama, the opening of new
sources was one, and chief among these, Spanish
sources. But to say, as has been hastily said, that
with Fletcher the contact of English drama with
that of Spain begins, is to say too much. The new
tragicomedy of Fletcher, in plays like *Philaster* and
its like, is often reported as Spanish in its anteced-
ents and as modelled on the fertile *comedia de
capa y espada* that flourished in the hands of Lope
de Vega, his contemporaries and successors. But
despite a certain general resemblance in romantic
content, the actual differences between Spanish
comedy and Fletcherian tragicomedy are at least as
great, and specific likenesses in plot, personage and

episode are as yet sadly to seek among the whisps
and gleanings of industrious workers in this attrac-
tive field. As to the whole matter, Dryden stated
the approximate truth when he said of dramatic
plots that "Beaumont and Fletcher had most of
theirs from Spanish novels." Some seventeen of the
fifty-two plays, commonly attributed to these authors, have been traced, in a greater or less indebted-
ness, to Spanish literature. Eighteen others remain
as yet unidentified as to source, and some of these
disclose a content and a manner not unlike the ruling traits of the drama of Spain. If we consider,
however, the almost incredible mass of the writings
of Lope de Vega (to mention him only), unread by
English and even by Spanish scholars, and further
keep in mind that those conversant with Spanish
drama are not always conversant with English and
vice versa, it would be rash to affirm that a last
word has been said on a topic which as yet has not
been seriously opened. So far as we now know,
Cervantes was Fletcher's favorite Spanish author,
and he seems to have been acquainted solely with
the Cervantes of prose. From that delightful collection of short stories, the *Exemplary Novels,* the
English poet drew the major plots of four dramas
and the underplot of *Rule a Wife and Have a Wife*
as well. Another play, *The Custom of the Country*
he derived from the last work of Cervantes, the
prose romance, *Persiles y Sigismunda.* As to *Don*

Quixote, apart from its suggestions at least for Beaumont's *Knight of the Burning Pestle* (a matter sometimes combatted),† the plots of no less than three other plays have been traced by various critics to the same immortal romance. Besides Cervantes, Fletcher drew upon Lope de Vega, on Juan de Flores, and on Gonzalo de Cespedes for four of his dramas. But not one of these originals is a play; nor need Fletcher have read a word of Spanish to have become acquainted with them; for all had been translated into French or English and were readily accessible to his hand.

About two only of the Fletcherian plays has any question on these points arisen. *Love's Cure,* first printed in the folio of 1647, but commonly dated back to the early years of King James, has been referred to a comedy by Guillen de Castro, written at so late a date as to make it quite unlikely that Fletcher could have seen it. Again, Fletcher's *Island Princess* has been referred to a source in the writings of the younger Argensola, not translated out of Spanish at such a date that it could have been known to Fletcher. But these matters are still under discussion, and on this particular subject we may take refuge in the judgment of Fitzmaurice-Kelly, the most eminent living authority on the literature of Spain, who writes: "Suffice it to say, at the

---

†R. M. Alden's ed. *Belles Lettres Series*, 1910, p. xxxviii.

present stage, the balance of probability is against the view that Fletcher knew Spanish."†

If we turn to other dramatists, we find an occasional contemporary of Fletcher following in his footsteps. *The Spanish Gipsy,* a tragicomedy of Middleton and Rowley, is made up of an effective combination of two stories of Cervantes. Rowley collaborated, too, with Fletcher in *The Maid in the Mill,* a comedy based on a story of Gonzalo de Cespedes, translated by Leonard Digges and called *Gerardo, the Unfortunate Spaniard.* Rowley's own powerful tragedy, *All's Lost by Lust,* draws on Spanish story, though his precise source remains problematic. Once more, *A Very Woman,* by Massinger, is derived from a story of the *Exemplary Novels.* The same dramatist's *Renegado* is said to be based on Cervantes *Los Baños de Argel,* and similarities have been traced between the same two authors in *The Fatal Dowery* and the interlude *El Viejo Celoso.* Moreover, it is said that neither of these Spanish pieces was translated in Massinger's life-time; although this is not certain. We may not feel sure that a Spanish play has actually influenced an English play by direct borrowing until we reach Shirley who is reported, on credible authority, to have utilized a comedy of Tirso de Molina in *The Opportunity,* and another of Lope de Vega in *The*

---

† Fitzmaurice-Kelly, as above, p. 23.

Young Admiral. Fitzmaurice-Kelly skeptically observes even as to these examples: "a minute demonstration of the extent of Shirley's borrowings would be still more satisfactory."

Passing by certain minor cases of questionable certainty, with Tuke's *Adventures of Five Hours,* written in 1662, and Digby's *Elvira, or the Worst Not Always True,* printed five years later, we reach unquestionable examples of the immediate adaptation of Spanish dramas to the English stage. This is not the place in which to dilate on the glories of the Spanish drama: the moral purpose of Alarcon, the brilliance and wit of Tirso de Molina, the happy fertility of Lope de Vega, the clarity of thought and lofty sentiment of Calderon, greatest of the Spanish dramatists. Both the comedies just mentioned are favorable specimens of the popular *comedias de capa y espada,* invented by Lope de Vega. Two ladies, a gallant and his friend, their lovers, a jealous brother or a difficult father with the attendant servants of all parties; mistake, accident, intrigue and involvement, honour touched and honour righted—such is the universal recipe of the comedy of cloak and sword. And here undoubtedly Spanish ideals had their effect with the not dissimilar ones of the contemporary French romances in hastening the transmutation of the tragicomedy of Fletcher into the absurdities and overwrought romanticism of the heroic play as successively written by Carlell, Davenant, Orrery and Dryden.

The coffers of Spanish drama, thus opened, continued to afford English playwrights their treasures. Dryden's *Rival Ladies* and an *Evening's Love or the Mock Astrologer* have been referred to Spanish sources: the last is Calderon by way of Corneille. Dryden's earliest dramatic effort, *The Wild Gallant,* has also been thought to be of Spanish origin. But this is an error, referable to a misreading of the prologue; the source is certainly English and doubtless Dryden's own invention. However, with the Earl of Orrery's *Guzman,* Mrs. Aphra Behn's *Dutch Lover* and *Rover* we are once more on certain Spanish ground; and thereafter Crowne, Wycherley, Cibber, Mrs. Centliver and even Steele drew not infrequently nor unsuccessfully on Spanish plot in an age quite beyond us.†

And now let us turn back to some Spanish influences of older time, not literary. It is well known that, contrary to the spirit of his people, King James, towards the close of his reign, drew towards a rapprochement with England's inveterate enemy. The Spanish ambassador, Gondomar, became a powerful personage at the English court; Sir Walter Raleigh, last of the old Elizabethan sea-dogs and long in prison, was sacrificed to the *entente cordiale*

---

† On Spanish influences in the later drama see the present writer's contribution to *The Cambridge History of English Literature,* viii, 124-132.

with Spain; and at length a marriage of Prince
Charles, heir to the crown, with the Infanta Maria
was not only projected but carried as far as a
journey to Spain by the Prince accompanied by the
favorite, Buckingham. The Spanish marriage was
unpopular in England from the first; and Spanish
delay and subterfuge, exorbitant demand and
slender fulfilment, at length forced even James definitely to abandon this unpopular and ill-advised
political alliance. It was at this juncture, in the
year 1624, that Thomas Middleton's audacious
satire in dramatic form, *A Game at Chess,* was
staged.† The play is a sustained allegory of the
political relations of a group of characters, figured
under the names of the various pieces of chess. The
stage was set for a field between the two houses,
black and white, but the order of the game was in
no wise preserved. King James and his late Queen,
the prince of Wales, Buckingham, and the Archbishop of Canterbury are figured as the king, queen,
duke, knight, and bishop of the white house. The
King and Queen of Spain, Olivares, the Spanish
king's chief minister, Gondomar, the recent Spanish ambassador at London, and the general of the
Jesuits were represented by the corresponding black
pieces. So far as there is any plot, the matter turns

---

†On this play see Bullen's prefatory note, his ed. of *Middleton,* vii. p. 3 ff. Also on the more general topic T. S. Graves,
The Political Use of the Stage, "Anglia," 1914.

on the machinations of the black house to over-
reach the white, in the course of which Gondomar is
mercilessly lampooned, and "the fat bishop," Antonio de Dominis, a renegade archbishop of the
Roman Church, later dean of Windsor, comes in
for a large share of raillery and satire. The visit
of Prince Charles is set forth in no doubtful terms,
although much else must remain to the modern
reader obscure. In the end the black king is check-
mated by "discovery," and swept with all his fellows into the bag. It cannot be said that the literary
value of Middleton's allegory is in any way remarkable. But its contemporary success was great. It
ran for nine days, an unusual period at the time,
and some of the actors reported that "they took
fifteen hundred pound." But their harvest was
brief. On information and complaint from the
Spanish ambassador, the actors were summoned
before the privy council, severely reprimanded, and
forbidden to act "any play or interlude whatso-
ever * * * until his majesty's pleasure be further
known." Middleton himself had meanwhile
"shifted out of the way." And King James, who
could not have been very seriously displeased, grac-
iously removed his interdict as to other plays soon
after. *A Game at Chess* stands alone as the only
attempt of the old English drama to emulate the
political satire of the comedies of Aristophanes,
although its essential features, the use of a game on

the stage, only too apparently to cloak a satirical or allegorical purpose, had long been known to English drama.

Another play, touching the Spanish peninsula and referable to the popular excitement of those same years, is one that has come down to us under the title *Believe as You List*, the work of Philip Massinger. The story, that of the enthusiastic Portuguese King Sebastian, who lost his life in 1578 at the battle of Alcazar in conflict with the Arabs, was old in the early years of King Charles; and it had already been treated several times on the stage. But the rise of several successive claimants for Sebastian's throne and the ruthless severity of the Spanish king in dealing with them, kept the subject ever new.† It appears that in 1631, Sir Henry Herbert, master of the revels and licenser of plays, had refused to license a play by Massinger "because it did contain dangerous matter as the deposing of Sebastian King of Portugal, by Philip, and there being a peace sworn betwixt the kings of England and Spain." This is almost certainly *Believe as You List* which the author cleverly transferred to ancient history, making the claimant for a throne supposedly long since slain in battle, Antiochus, King of Lower Asia, and the power that frustrated

---

†The immediate source is a tract entitled *The Strangest Adventure That Ever Happened*, translated from the French by Anthony Munday, 1601, but ultimately of Spanish origin.

his ambition and sent him a broken and pathetic figure, a slave to the galleys, the impersonal power of Rome. It is with the following clever caveat that the playwright disarms his lynx-eyed censor:

If you find what's Roman here,
Grecian or Asiatic, draw too near
A late and sad example, 'tis confessed
He's but an English scholar at his best,
A stranger to cosmography, and may err
In the countries' names, the shape and character
Of the persons he presents.

To summarize these somewhat desultory paragraphs: Spanish literary influences on the drama in Tudor times were slight and confined, almost entirely, to an occasional plot, derived as a rule through a French or English translation as an intermediary. In the reign of James, Beaumont and Fletcher, Massinger, and William Rowley, alone among the dramatists of note, drew on Spanish sources for their plays; and though the question cannot be regarded as definitely settled, it seems likely that their sources lay wholly in fiction, translated into other and to them more familiar languages of the continent or into English. In the reign of King Charles I, the relations of England and Spain became closer, and it was then that Spanish drama for the first time came into touch with the English stage. That touch was closest at the Restoration, when the cavalier returned with his foreign luggage, and the taste of the king conspired with the experiences of his courtiers to foster many experiments. But Spanish influence was soon eclipsed by that of France, aided by the strong national spirit that prolonged the influence of Jonson and his contemporaries for generations after their decease.

Two questions may perhaps here arise to those who have followed this quest of ours for scources classical, Italian, French and Spanish: first were there no other foreign influences on this old drama of England? and secondly, what was there left that was native after all this use of the coin of other realms? As to other foreign influences, there were the Low Countries, near to England as to France, and one of the three allies, the English, the Dutch and the winds, that had scattered the Spanish Armada and strewn the wrecks of noble galleons from Cornwall to the Hebrides. And deeper to the east there was what the Elizabethans called "High Almain," a land of many states and principalities, where arts flourished and where there were noble universities, such as that of Wittenberg where Dr. Faustus had carried on his nefarious dealings in the black art by forbidden study, and whence Hamlet, the Prince of Denmark, had returned to avenge that foul and most unnatural murder in the kings' castle at Elsinore. The actual literary influences between the Teutonic continent and England at best are few; in the drama, they are scattered and often problematic.† In earlier Tudor times, when Holbein, was painting English princes and Brandt's *Narrenschiff* had become a work of international repute, the Dutch and German humanistic drama exerted an appreciable influence on the English morality, whether *Everyman* is the English version of a Dutch original or *vice versa* as a civil Dutch scholar would have us believe. *Acolastus,* in Palsgrave's school version, and the *Studentes* of Stymmelius, famous humanist dramas both of them, appear to have been well known in the times of Henry and his son. And several early English plays, such as *Misogonus, The Nice Wanton* and others may be named as of this kindred. Gascoigne's *Glass of Government,* 1566, seems plainly a school drama, brought back from Holland by that old soldier in his knapsack; but no one has as yet found the original Dutch owner.‡ Twenty years later Marlowe's celebrated *Doctor Faustus,* and a line of interesting English dramas after it, were inspired by

---

†The authority on this topic is C. H. Herford, *Studies in the Literary Relations of England and Germany in the Sixteenth Century,* to which may be added the chapter on "German History im English Literature" by G. Waterhouse, *The Literary Relations of England and Germany in the Seventeeth Century,* 1914.

‡See Herford, p. 158 ff and Bond, *Early Plays from the Italian,* p. ci ff.

the old German *Faustbuch*. Moreover the inexorable stubbornness of dates compels us to declare that as to the Faust legend, Goethe was fired by Marlowe, not Marlowe by Goethe. The story of Fortunatus, his inexhaustible purse and wishing-cap, so delightfully dramatized by Dekker in his *Old Fortunatus*, 1596, may have come to England by way of the German *Volksbuch* of that tale. But the story shows traces of a romance origin or transition at the least. Heroes such as Faust and Fortunatus wander far. An humbler cousin-german who perks his impudent face into Elizabethan literature is Eulenspiegel, translated Howleglass by Ben Jonson and introduced into the antimasque of *The Fortunate Isles*, one of his later masques at court. But so far as is known Eulenspiegel never obtruded his whole person into an English play.†

A personage, also of German extraction, is Friar Rush who played a more important part, appearing in at least two English plays, one of them extant, and inspiring a third. *Friar Rush, and the Proud Woman of Amsterdam*, 1601, of Henslowe's mention is lost; but Dekkers' *If this be not a Good Play, the Devil is in it*, 1612, details in full the legend of the wicked friar who poisoned a whole monastery, and Jonson's *The Devil is an Ass*, 1616, although dependent on the Italian story of Belfegor,

†On this topic see W. D. Brie *Eulenspiegel in England*, "Palaestra," xxviii, 1902.

shows familiarity with the Rush legend. As regards
to language there is some acceptable Dutch in
Dekker's charming comedy of London life, *The
Shoemakers' Holiday*, 1599; and Elze long ago
praised the fluent German of that problematic
tragedy, *Alphonsus of Germany*, a play as doubtful
as to date as to authorship. But these things prove
little. With the German Steel Yard, the recognized
haunt of German merchants in London, and the
considerable trade with the Hanseatic towns,
neither the language nor the manners of "High
Almain" could have been unknown to the Elizabethans. Many high-born German travellers—when
have Germans not travelled?—came to England,
and some have left us precious legacies as to what
they saw; for they were as observant, as intent on
the use of their opportunities, as well informed, and
as literal in their interpretations of what they saw
as their fellow-countrymen remain to the present
day.† One of these travellers, it may be recalled,
is identified with a certain Count Mompelgard, actually Frederick, Duke of Wirtemberg, who visited
England in 1592. He is alluded to in *The Merry
Wives of Windsor* as having, with two attedants,
"cosened all the hosts of Reading, of Maidenhead,

---

†On German travellers in England, see W. B. Rye, *England
as Seen by Foreigners*, 1865; and G. Binz, *Deutsche Besucher
im Shakespearischen London*, "Beilage zur Allgemeine Zei-
tung," Munich, Aug., 1902.

of Colebrook of horses and money;" and, throwing
"me off from behind one of them in a slough of
mire," says Falstaff's veracious Bardolf, they "set
spurs and away, like three German devils, three
Doctor Faustuses."† But here assuredly is a foreign influence which, however dramatic, is not
literary.

Among matters historical, a line of plays extend
from the early *Doctor Dodypoll,* the scene of which
is the court of Saxony, and *A Larum for London,* a
news-play dealing with the sack of Antwerp, to several dramas of a genuine interest from a literary
point of view or to the history of the drama. For
example, Henry Chettle's *Hoffman,* much of the
scene of which lies near Lubeck, is one of the striking series of tragedies of revenge, among which
Danish *Hamlet,* is the chief. In *The Hector of
Germany,* the wranglings of the electors of the empire at an indeterminable date take the scenes straggling over half the continent of Europe. *A Defi-
ance of Fortune,* 1590, and *Evoradanus, Prince of
Denmark,* 1595, are romances merely Teutonic in
location. *Alphonsus of Germany,* which is certainly
not work of Chapman, has been thought from the
idiomatic German of certain passages to have had a
German collaborator; and Professor Parrott sug-

---

†IV. v. 61. The first quarto reads in this passage: "There
is three sorts of cosen garmobles;" with which compare
"Mompelgard."

gests Weckerlin whose services with the Duke of Wirtemburg in England, 1608, association with the Palsgrave Frederick, husband of the Princess Elizabeth, and fluency in verse in both languages is well known. It is interesting to note in this connection that the story of the Capture of Stuhl-Weissenburg by the Turks was dramatised with its recapture by the Christians. Infinitely above such productions is Fletcher's fine tragedy on *Sir John von Olden Barnavelt*, 1620, in which the almost contemporary struggle between that able statesman—in the play misrepresented—and Maurice of Nassau is set forth with realistic effect. A later and inferior tragedy dealing with more strictly a German theme and one almost equally contemporary was Henry Glapthorne's *Wallenstein*, 1629, or later. This play has naturally attracted much attention in Germany; but the author was unequal to this great subject so much later to be treated by Schiller. It is of interest to learn that Glapthorne's tragedy was acted in Germany in 1666 and again in 1690. The material in the cases of plays such as these is usually a newspamphlet translated out of the original tongue. In no case, save one and but for *Faustus* and perhaps *Fortunatus*, can we find the employment of a strictly Teutonic legend as material for a play, and that is the underplot of a tragedy of a title unpronounceable by polite lips wherein is employed the venerable story of the wicked Bishop Hatto and the

Mouse Tower in the Rhine.† The romantic major plot of this play in which figures a Duke of Saxony, has been taken over from a novel by Greene, *Planetomachia*.

Of very truth in this subject of the relations of England and Germany in the drama of the sixteenth and seventeenth centuries, the current was not from Germany to England but from England to Germany. As far back as Shakespeare's early youth companies of English players had acted in Germany, and troupe after troupe followed, acting at Dresden, Vienna, Frankfurt and elsewhere, as far north as Denmark and as far south as Gratz in Austria.‡ In that delectable book, *The Itinerary of Fynes Moryson,* a scholar of Cambridge, who held a traveling scholarship and used it as few have used such opportunities since, there is the following passage which the pride of a man who had seen Shakespeare's plays acted in Shakespeare's own lifetime may extenuate: "Germany hath some few wandering comedians, more deserving pity than praise; for the serious parts are dully penned and worse acted, and the mirth they make is ridiculous and nothing less than witty. So as I remember that when some of our cast, despised stage players came

---

†*The Costly Whore*, Bullen's *Old English Plays*, iv.

‡See especially E. Herz, *Englische Schauspieler und Englisches Schauspiel zur zeit Shakespeare's in Deutschland*, 1903.

out of England into Germany and played at Frankfurt in the time of the mart, having neither a complete number of actors nor any good apparel nor any
ornament of the stage, yet the Germans, not understanding a word they said, both men and women,
flocked wonderfully to see their gesture and action
rather than hear them speaking English which they
understood not, and pronouncing pieces and patches
of English plays which myself and some Englishmen there present could not hear without great
wearisomeness. Yea myself coming from Frankfurt, in the company of some chief marchants,
Dutch and Flemish, heard them often brag of the
good market they had made, only condoling that
they had not the leisure to hear the English players."‡ More than this, the repertory of the German
stage in Shakespeare's time and for a couple of
generations after was partly English. There was a
*Tragoedia der bestrafte Brudermord oder Prinz
Hamlet aus Dännemark;* there was *eine sehr kläg-
liche Tragoedia von Tito Andronico;* and the
Tragoedia von Romio und Julietta. Outside of
Shakespeare there was a *Comoedia von Fortunato
und seinem Seckel und Wünschütlein* (Dekker's *Old
Fortunatus); eine shöne lustige comoedia von Je-
mand und Nemandt* (the well known English

---

‡*Shakespeare's Europe*, Unpublished Chapters of Fynes
Moryson's *Itinerary*, ed. C. E. Hughes, 1903, p. 304.

Somebody and Nobody) and many more, all of them translations of popular Elizabethan plays.†

Most of these plays were gathered into a precious manuscript, about 1620, offering us much thought and food for speculation as to the international dramatic relations of these old times. It is good to think of Goethe and Schiller, lighting the fires of their genius at the altars of Marlowe and Shakespeare as of the lesser Klopstock, paying the tribute of imitation in his *Messias* to Milton's to him unapproachable *Paradise Lost.* These things should make us who speak the tongue of Shakespeare—however otherwise than he spoke it—feel less young, less diffidant, less dubious of the priceless heritage which after all is ours, and not his who speaks an alien language however rich its own treasures.

And now as to our other question: What does this foreign debt of our old English drama really come to? Here was Jonson guilty of getting away with practically all the Latin and Greek classics, but using them with a fine discretion and giving us out of their metal current coin of his own minting. Here was Shakespeare with his "small Latin and less Greek," innocent of such grand larceny, yet not hesitating to take his own whether he found it pre-

---

†See A. Cohn, *Shakespeare in Germany,* 1865, in which these old plays are reprinted in English translation.

viously purloined in North's *Plutarch,* Painter's *Palace of Pleasure* or Holinshed's *Chronicles of England, Ireland and Scotland.* Marston knew Italian, and his plays are the worse for it; Massinger and Shirley may have read Spanish, and not much did it help them. The use of French models for tragedy kept Daniel and Greville apparently oblivious of the great popular dramatic literature that flourished about them, however French subjects, imbibed through translation, may have spurred the genius of Chapman. In the days of our old triumphant drama the beautiful myths and stories, the chaste and restrained style, the earnest and lofty ideals of ancient literature guided the wandering renaissance spirit as all these noble things have guided mankind wherever learning and the love of learning have flourished. On a lower plain, but often more directly, Italian, French and Spanish fiction were drawn upon by many of our dramatists with address and effect, the histories of these countries to an appreciable but to a less degree. And the wonder of it all is that there was so little actual contact of drama with drama. The only actual touch of play with play was in the case of Seneca and Plautus, the academic tragedy of France and the Italian dramas of the *coterie,* naturally the models of court and university circles. For the influence of popular Spanish drama on the popular stage of England we must wait until well into the reign of King

Charles I; for the influence of popular French drama, until the Restoration brought back the noble and gentle exiles to revel in the court of his dissolute son and successor.

What was there left that was native after all this use of the coin of other realms? Nearly everything is left. For how English after all is the fiber of our old drama, its pictures of the old ways, of the old London manners, its pageantry of the old chivalry, its honest fear of God and respect for man; and how universal it is at its best in that the spaciousness and liberal spirit of this old age has come to be the spirit dominating and setting an example to our own later times. Literature knows no ethics finer than those of Shakespeare and his fellows, judged in the large; nor any poetry more witching, more ideally beautiful, more universally successful in its time, more truly noble, more potently elevating. There were ugly things in the old days, as there are, alas, in these; and there were failures then as now. But how many were the successes, and what a precious body of imperishable art these great dramatists from Lyly and Marlowe to Ford and Shirley, have left to successive times. Feeling as I do that there is nothing foreign and alien in literature as between England and our own native America, let me apply to Elizabethan drama in general and in despite of all these foreign influences, the words of the late Dr. Horace Howard

Furness in another application: "It is through and through an English [drama], on English soil, in English air, beneath English oaks; and it will be loved and admired, cherished and appreciated by English [speaking] men [and women] as long as an English word is uttered by an English tongue."

A SELECT BIBLIOGRAPHY

*of books and articles treating Foreign Influences in
Elizabethan Drama, excluding works on the History
of the Drama and, for the most part, Introductions
and other apparatus appended to Texts of plays,
in all of which much additional material may, of
course, be found.*

I. Among older discussions of the influences
of the classics, may be mentioned that of F. W.
Farrar, *The Influences of the Revival of Classical
Studies on English Literature during the Reigns of
Elizabeth and James,* 1856. For Seneca, see J. W.
Cunliffe, *The Influence of Seneca on Elizabethan
Tragedy,* 1893; and the same author's *Early English Classical Tragedies,* Introduction, 1912. Kindred discussion is contained in R. Fischer, *Zur
Kunstentwicklung der englischen Tragödie,* 1893;
in A. H. Thorndike, "Tragedy," *Types of English
Literature,* 1908; the same author's "The Relations
of Hamlet to Contemporary Revenge Plays," *Publications of the Modern Language Association,*
1902; and F. W. Moorman, "The Pre-Shakespear-
ean Ghost," *Modern Language Review,* 1906. On
the general influence of Plautus, K. von Reinhard-
stöttner, *Plautus spätere Bearbeitungen plautinischen*

Kunstspiele, 1886; M. W. Wallace, Introduction to *The Birthe of Hercules,* 1903, treats of Plautine influence in the sixteenth century, direct and indirect; C. C. Coulter, in *The Journal of English and Germanic Philology,* 1920, of "The Plautine Tradition in Shakespeare;" and P. J. Enk, of "Shakespeare's direct debt" to Plautus, in *Neophilologus,* 1920. Several Latin plays by English academic authors, modeled on Seneca and Plautus (as on other models) are described by G. B. Churchill and W. Keller in the *Shakespeare-Jahrbuch,* 1898; and F. S. Boas admirably discusses *University Drama,* 1914, within the Tudor age. The extremes of date, as of opinion, on this subject are R. Farmer, *On the Learning of Shakespeare,* 1767, and J. C. Collins, "Shakespeare as a Classical Scholar" in *Studies in Shakespeare,* 1904. A valuable literary discussion is that of P. Stapfer, *Shakespeare and Classical Antiquity,* translation by E. J. Carey, 1880; recent contributions are, E. Wolfhardt, *Shakespeare und das Griechentum,* Berlin Dissertation, 1920; and the renewed discussion of Shakespeare's Latin by E. A. Sonnenschein and Mrs. C. C. Stopes in the *Times Literary Suppliment,* March and April, 1921. Besides more general works, see as to Jonson, E. Koeppel, "Quellen-studien zu den Dramen Jonson's, *"Quellen und Forschungen,* 1895; R. Aronstein, "Jonson's Theorie des Lustspiele," *Anglia,* 1895; E. Woodbridge, *Studies in the Comedies of Jonson,*

1898. See also W. D. Briggs, "Cynthia's Revels and Seneca," *Flügel Memorial Volume*, 1917; and W. P. Mustard, "Notes on Ben Jonson's Catiline," *Modern Language Notes*, 1921.

II. As to Italian influences see J. R. Murray, *The Influence of Italian upon English Literature during the Sixteenth and Seventeenth Centuries*, 1886; M. A. Scott, "Elizabethan Translations from the Italian," *Publications of the Modern Language Association*, 1895-1899, revised edition 1916; the same author's "The Elizabethan Drama especially in its relations to the Italian of the Renaissance," Yale Thesis, 1894; and L. Einstein, *The Italian Renaissance in England*, 1902, a work largely indebted to the other two. E. Meyer, treats of "Machiavelli and the Elizabethan Drama," *Litterarhistorische Forschungen*, 1897. On the sources of English plays in the Italian *novelle*, see especially E. Koeppel, "Studien zur Geschichte der italienischen Novelle in der englischen Litteratur des sechzehnten Jahrhunderts," *Quellen und Forschungen*, 1892; the same author's "Zur Quellen-Kunde des Stuart's Drama," *Archiv für das Studium der neueren Sprachen*, 1895-1897; L. L. Schuecking, *Studien über die stofflichen Beziehungen der englischen Komödie zur italienischen bis Lilly*, 1901; A. Ott, *Die italienische Novelle in englischen Drama von 1600 bis zur Restauration*, 1904; and R. W. Bond, "Introductory Essay" to *Early Plays from the Italian*, 1911, an excellent piece of work. See also J. W. Cunliffe, "The Influence of Italian in early Elizabethan Drama," *Modern Philology,* 1906-1907; W. Smith, "Italian and English Comedy," *Modern Philology,* 1908; and L. Collison-Morley, *Shakespeare in Italy.* 1920. On the pastoral, see W. W. Greg, *Pastoral Poetry and Pastoral Drama,* 1906, an authoritative work; and H. Smith, "Pastoral Influence in English Drama," *Pennsylvania Thesis,* 1899. Also J. Laidler, "A History of the Pastoral Drama in England," *Englische Studien,* 1905; A. H. Thorndike, "The Pastoral Element in English Drama before 1605," *Modern Language Notes,* 1900, and J. W. Cunliffe, "Italian Prototypes of the Masque and Dumb Show," *Publications of the Modern Language Association,* 1907.

III. The most recent work on French influences is that of S. Lee, *The French Renaissance in England,* 1910, to be used with caution. See also A. H. Upham, *The French Influence in English Literature,* 1908; and J. W. Cunliffe, "Early French Tragedy in the Light of Recent Scholarship," *Journal of Comparative Literature,* 1903. On the historical plays see F. E. Schelling, *The English Chronicle Play,* 1902. French Seneca is discussed by J. A. Lester in *Connections between the Drama of France and Great Britain particularly in the Elizabethan Period,* Harvard Thesis, unpublished, 1902, and by M. W.

Croll, *The Works of Fulke Greville,* Pennsylvania Thesis, 1903. See also F. S. Boas, "The Sources of Chapman's Conspiracy of Byron," *Athenaeum,* January, 1903; his "Edward Grimestone, Translator," *Modern Philology,* 1906; and E. Lehman, Introduction to his edition of *Chabot, Admiral of France,* Pennsylvania Thesis, 1906. This subject is well summarized by T. M. Parrott in his edition of *Chapman,* 1910; and see also F. L. Schoell, in *Revue Germanique,* 1913, and Introduction to his edition of *Charlemagne,* 1920. Two recent contributions on Florio are L. Chambrun, *Giovanni Florio,* Paris, 1921; and J. M. Murray, "Shakespeare and Florio," *Nation and Athenaeum,* XXIX.

IV. On general Spanish influences see J. G. Underhill, *Spanish Literature in the England of the Tudors,* 1899; J. Fitzmaurice-Kelly, *The Relations between Spanish and English Literature,* Liverpool, 1910, an excellent pamphlet; and the introduction to the same author's translation of the *Exemplary Novels* of Cervantes, 1902. Among the many articles on the Spanish sources of individual plays may be mentioned that of A. Stiefel, "Die Nachahmung spanischer Komoedien in England," *Archiv,* 1897; and A. S. W. Rosenbach, "The Curious Impertinent in English Drama," *Modern Language Notes,* 1902, part of a larger and yet unpublished study on "Spanish Sources of Beaumont and Fletcher." See also the same author's "The In-

fluence of the *Celestina* in Early English Drama,"
Shakespeare-Jahrbuch, 1903. Koeppel in his
"Quellen-Studien," *Münchener Beiträge,* 1895, has
gathered together most of the older attributions of
Spanish source. There are also several paragraphs
on Spanish influences on English drama by the
present writer in the eighth volume of the *Cambridge
History of English Literature,* 1912. A worker in
the field of specific resemblances between English
and Spanish drama is J. de Perott, see *Publications
of Clark University,* 1905, and elsewhere. J. P.
Wickersham Crawford treats, in *Modern Language
Notes,* June, 1920, "A Sixteenth-Century Spanish
Analogue of *Measure for Measure."* See also R.
Grossmann, "Spanien und das Elizabethanische
Drama," *Hamburgische Universität Abhandlung.*
Bd. 4, 1920; and H. Thomas, *Shakespeare and
Spain,* 1922.

Earlier German relations are best studied in
C. H. Herford, *Studies in the Literary Relations of
England and Germany in the Sixteenth Century,*
1888, an excellent work. G. Waterhouse, *The Literary Relations of England and Germany in the
Seventeenth Century,* 1914, adds little; Wallace,
The Birthe of Hercules and Bond, *Early Plays from
the Italian,* both mentioned above, touch likewise
this subject. On the relations of the Faust story,
see A. W. Ward in his edition of Marlowe's *Faustus*
and Greene's *Friar Bacon,* third ed. 1892; on the

Fortunatus story, Valentin Schmidt; and the Introduction to the ed. of that play in *Deutsche Dichter des sechzehnten Jahrhunderts,* vol. 13; W. D. Brie, on "Eulenspiegel in England," *Palaestra,* 1902. See also Herford, for the references to Friar Rush; and G. L. Kittredge, *Publications of the Modern Language Association,* 1900. W. P. Frijlink, in her edition of *Barnavelt,* Amsterdam, 1922, discusses the relations of that drama to Dutch history. Finally E. Herz, *Englische Schauspieler und englisches Schauspiel zur zeit Shakespeares in Deutschland,* 1903, well treats its title subject; and A. Cohn, *Shakespeare in Germany,* 1865, reprints several old German plays of English origin for the curious.

INDEX

A

Acolastus, 7, 8, 129
Addison, Joseph, *Cato*, 87
Aeschylus, 33
Agricola, George, 5
Alabaster, William, *Roxana*, 73
Alden, R. M., 120
Alexander, Sir William, *Monarchic Tragedies*, 87; *Alphonsus of Germany*, 131, 132
Amyot, Jacques, 82
Argensola, Bartolomeo de, 120
Ariosto, Lodovico, *I Suppositi*, 47, 59; *Orlando Furioso*, 49.
Aristophanes, 21, 23, 33, 125; *Plutus*, 5; *Pax*, 5
Aristotle, 19, 30
Ascham, Roger, 7, 19, 39, 49, 62
Aubrey, John, 29, 30

B

Bacon, Francis, 18
Bagehot, Walter, 33

Bale, John, 5
Bandello, Matteo, 44, 50, 51, 54, 55, 64, 66, 69
Barnes, Barnabe, 20, 58
Beard, Thomas, 64
Beaton, Cardinal, 6
Beaumont, Francis, 61, 117, 118, 127; *The Knight of the Burning Pestle*, 71, 120
Behn, Aphra, *The Dutch Lover, The Rover*, 123
Belleforest, François de, 51, 55, 64; *Histories Tragiques*, 54
Berners, Lord, 77
Binz, G., 131
Boas, F. S., 6, 13, 47, 95
Boccaccio, 50, 60; *Decameron*, 59, 61; *Ameto*, 69
Boisteau de Launai, Pierre, 51, 54
Bond, R. W., 47, 129
Boisteau, 51, 54
Bradley, Dr., of Edinburgh, 74
Brandon, Samuel, *Virtuous Octavia*, 84
Brandt, Sebastian, 129
Brie, W. D., 130

INDEX

INDEX

INDEX

THE END